I1007675

50 Walks
HISTORY

Produced by AA Publishing
© Automobile Association Developments Limited 2007
Illustrations © Automobile Association Developments Limited 2007

Published by AA Publishing (a trading name of Automobile
Association Developments Limited, whose registered office is Fanum
House, Basing View, Basingstoke, Hampshire RG21 4EA;
registered number 1878835)

This product includes mapping data licensed
from Ordnance Survey® with the permission of
the Controller of Her Majesty's Stationery
Office. © Crown copyright 2007. All rights
reserved. Licence number 1878835

ISBN 978-0-7495-5550-4

A03033e

A CIP catalogue record for this book is available
from the British Library.

The contents of this book are believed correct at the time of printing.
Nevertheless, the publishers cannot be held responsible for any errors
or omissions or for changes in the details given in this book or for
the consequences of any reliance on the information it provides. We
have tried to ensure accuracy in this book, but things do change and
we would be grateful if readers would advise us of any inaccuracies
they may encounter.

We have taken all reasonable steps to ensure that these walks are
safe and achievable by walkers with a realistic level of fitness.
However, all outdoor activities involve a degree of risk and the
publishers accept no responsibility for any injuries caused to
readers whilst following these walks. For more advice on walking
safely see opposite.

Some of the walks may appear in other AA publications.

Visit the AA Publishing website at www.theAA.com

Colour reproduction by Keene Group, Andover
Printed in China by Everbest Printing Company Ltd

Walking in Safety

All these walks are suitable for any reasonably fit person, but less experienced walkers should try the easier walks first. Route finding is usually straightforward, but you will find that an Ordnance Survey map is a useful addition to the route maps and descriptions.

Risks

Although each walk here has been researched with a view to minimising the risks to the walkers who follow its route, no walk in the countryside can be considered to be completely free from risk. Walking in the outdoors will always require a degree of common sense and judgement to ensure that it is as safe as possible.

- Be particularly careful on cliff paths and in upland terrain, where the consequences of a slip can be very serious.

- Remember to check tidal conditions before walking on the seashore.

- Some sections of route are by, or cross, busy roads. Take care and remember traffic is a danger even on minor country lanes.

- Be careful around farmyard machinery and livestock, especially if you have children with you.

- Be aware of the consequences of changes in the weather and check the forecast before you set out. Carry spare clothing and a torch if you are walking in the winter months. Remember the weather can change very quickly at any time of the year, and in moorland and heathland areas, mist and fog can make route finding much harder. Don't set out in these conditions unless you are confident of your navigation skills in poor visibility. In summer remember to take account of the heat and sun; wear a hat and carry spare water.

- On walks away from centres of population you should carry a whistle and survival bag. If you do have an accident requiring the emergency services, make a note of your position as accurately as possible and dial 999.

Legend & map

Legend

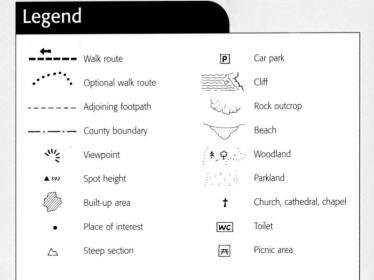

← – – – – –	Walk route	P	Car park
⋯⋯⋯	Optional walk route		Cliff
– – – – – –	Adjoining footpath		Rock outcrop
– · – · – · –	County boundary		Beach
⁀	Viewpoint		Woodland
▲ 392	Spot height		Parkland
	Built-up area	✝	Church, cathedral, chapel
•	Place of interest	WC	Toilet
△	Steep section	⊞	Picnic area

Legend & map

locator map

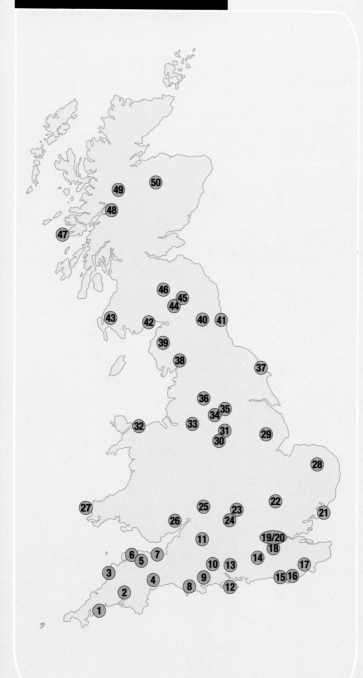

Contents

Contents *(vertical, left margin)*

Contents

Rating: Each walk is rated for its relative difficulty compared to the other walks in this book. Walks marked 🚶🚶 🚶 are likely to be shorter and easier with little total ascent. The hardest walks are marked 🚶🚶 🚶🚶 🚶🚶 .

Walking in Safety: For advice and safety tips see page 3

Introduction

Landscape historians are fond of calling the British landscape a palimpsest – a manuscript on which old writing has been constantly overwritten by new. And it's a pretty accurate way of describing the manner in which each succeeding generation and era has left behind its own legacy in the landscape – if you know how to read it.

The man who did most to help us read the landscape, and the founding father of the discipline now taught in universities across the country, was Professor W G Hoskins. In his seminal *The Making of the English Landscape*, first published in 1955 and still in print, he neatly summarised his findings in the phrase: "Everything is older than we think."

But modern landscape research, linked to archaeology, geophysics and aerial photography, means that we are constantly learning more, to the extent that Professor Hoskins' original view that the landscape of today was largely the product of the last 1,500 years has been revised back in time by a factor of almost ten. Today you could almost say: "Everything is even older than we thought."

These 50 family-length walks will take past six millennia of Britain's history, from the Neolithic temples of the Avebury stone circle in Wiltshire (where, unlike the cordoned-off megaliths of better-known Stonehenge, you can actually touch the stones), to following in the 'hot trod' hoofprints of the 16th-century cattle-rustling reivers at Newcastleton on the Scottish Borders in Walk 44.

As Professor Hoskins also observed, field walking is by far the best and most rewarding way of coming to terms with the landscape history of Britain. So when, for example, you undertake the ascent of the lonely headland of Dodman Point in Cornwall in Walk 1, you will pass through Iron Age and medieval field systems before reaching the 18th-century Watch House on your way to The Bulwark, which marks the defensive embankment of the 2,000-year-old Iron Age promontory fort on the headland. That's two thousand years in just over four miles.

And Dodman Point is not an exceptional example of the time-travelling you can do by following the walks in this book. Take Walk 40, a 6-mile (9.7km) stroll from the Roman town of Corbridge (*Corstopitum*) in Northumberland, once the most northerly settlement in the mighty Roman Empire. Although the Romans were here first, it was the Saxons who founded the modern town, and the parish church has Saxon foundations. Two pele towers remind you of the troubled Border Wars of the Middle Ages, and you'll pass the converted barns where modern best-selling author Catherine Cookson once lived.

Another historic literary connection is made in Walk 46, which visits the ruins of Dryburgh Abbey in Dumfries and Galloway, the last resting place of Sir Walter Scott, whose 19th-century novels played a part in the rivival of interest in Scottish culture. After the pleasant, 4½ mile (7.2km) walk, you can drink the creator of *Ivanhoe*'s health at the Dryburgh Abbey Hotel.

Myths and folklore feature strong in our history, and Walk 33 will take you into the realms of Arthurian legend with an easy, 3-mile (4.8km) ascent of Alderley Edge on the Cheshire edge of the Peak District. Mining of copper and lead has gone on here in adits beneath the sandstone edge for at least 4,000 years, but the most famous legend relates to the Wizard's Well, where a hidden cave is said to be guarded by a wizard whom some people think is Arthur's wise old mentor, Merlin.

Another legendary figure of British prehistory is Boudica, Queen of the Iceni, who rose up against the invading Romans in AD 60 and laid waste to the towns of Colchester, London and St Albans. Walk 28, from Caistor St Edmund in Norfolk, takes you on a 6¼ mile (10.1km) hike along part of Boudica's Way from the site of the Roman cantonal capital of *Venta Icenorum*, where the ill-fated Boudican rebellion began.

And you can visit the site of a rare Romano-Celtic temple – where the Romans apparently hedged their bets by worshipping both pagan and Christian gods – on a 5-mile (8km) tramp along the high and breezy Greensand ridge of Farley Heath in Surrey in Walk 14.

Using this Book

Information panels
A panel for each walk shows its relative difficulty, the distance and total amount of ascent. An indication of the gradients you will encounter is shown by the rating ▲▲ ▲▲ ▲▲ (no steep slopes) to ▲▲ ▲▲ ▲▲ (several very steep slopes).

Maps
Each of the 50 walks in this book has its own map, with the walk route clearly marked with a hatched line. Some can be extended by following an extra section of route marked with a dotted line, but for reasons of space, instructions for the extensions are not given in the text. The minimum time suggested for the walk is for reasonably fit walkers and doesn't allow for stops. Each walk has a suggested large-scale OS map which should be used in conjunction with the walk route map. Laminated aqua3 maps are longer lasting and water resistant.

Start Points
The start of each walk is given as a six-figure grid reference prefixed by two letters indicating which 100km square of the National Grid it refers to. You'll find more information on grid references on most Ordnance Survey maps.

Dogs
We have tried to give dog owners useful advice about how dog friendly each walk is. Please respect other countryside users. Keep your dog under control, especially around livestock, and obey local bylaws and other dog control notices.

Car Parking
Many of the car parks suggested are public, but occasionally you may find you have to park on the roadside or in a lay-by. Please be considerate when you leave your car, ensuring that access roads or gates are not blocked and that other vehicles can pass safely.

Ancient Walls on the Lonely Dodman

A circuit of the headland of Dodman Point, where Iron Age people established a fortified encampment.

•DISTANCE•	4½ miles (7.2km)
•MINIMUM TIME•	3hrs
•ASCENT / GRADIENT•	377ft (115m) ▲▲▲
•LEVEL OF DIFFICULTY•	🚶 🚶 🚶
•PATHS•	Good coastal paths. Inland paths can be muddy, 9 stiles
•LANDSCAPE•	Open fields and coastal cliffs
•SUGGESTED MAP•	aqua3 OS Explorer 105 Falmouth & Mevagissey
•START / FINISH•	Grid reference: SX 011415
•DOG FRIENDLINESS•	Dogs on lead through grazed areas
•PARKING•	Gorran Haven car park, pay at kiosk
•PUBLIC TOILETS•	Gorran Haven

BACKGROUND TO THE WALK

The high and lonely headland of Dodman Point thrusts its great bulk into the sea near Mevagissey and Gorran Haven, forming the eastern arch of Veryan Bay, on the south coast of Cornwall. Local people make no bones about the name. To them this dark and brooding promontory has always been the 'Deadman'. It was recorded as such on old maps. The source of the name may be prosaic, of course, a probable distortion of an ancient Cornish word; but 'Deadman' strikes a suitably menacing echo with the nearby Vault Beach and with the threatening names of such tideline rocks as the Bell and Mean-lay that lie at the base of the 328ft (100m) Dodman cliffs. By whatever name, the Dodman is a natural fortress, and across its broad shoulders lies a massive earthen embankment, the landward defences of a 'promontory fort'. This is one of a number of such protected farm settlements that dates back to the Cornish Iron Age.

Vault Beach

The first part of the walk leads from the village of Gorran Haven along the coastal footpath to the great sweep of Vault Beach, or Bow Beach, as it is also known. From above the beach the path rises steadily to the broad-backed promontory of the Dodman. The headland is crowned with a sepulchral granite cross placed there in 1896 by the Reverend George Martin, Rector of nearby St Michael Caerhays. Whether or not the cross was placed as a navigation aid or as a religious gesture is not entirely clear. The inscription on the cross argues for Martin's religious certainties above all. Just inland from the cross (see Directions Point ④), but hidden by scrub, is the Dodman Watch House, a charming survivor of the late 18th century. This much restored little building was an Admiralty signal station, part of a chain of similar structures along the English Channel Coast. It was used in later years by coastguards and has been restored by the National Trust.

From the Dodman, the route follows the coast path for a short distance along the headland's western flank to where a gate allows access to fields that bear the vestigial marks of prehistoric and medieval cultivation systems. On the main route, you turn off the coast path here to follow the line of a great Iron Age earthwork, known as the Bulwark. This is an impressive piece of engineering, even by today's standards, some 2,000ft (609m) in length and over 12ft (4m) high. Eventually a track leads to the serene hamlet of Penare and then across fields and down a little valley back into Gorran Haven.

Walk 1 **Directions**

① Turn left on leaving the car park and walk down to **Gorran Haven** harbour. Just before the access to the beach, turn right up **Fox Hole Lane**, then go up steps, signposted '**Vault Beach**'. Go up more steps, and then through a gate. Follow the coast path ahead, past a sign for the National Trust property of **Lamledra**.

② Keep left at a junction below a rocky outcrop. A steep alternative path leads up right from here, past a memorial plaque, to rejoin the main coast path. On the main route however go down some stone steps and follow the path along the slope. At a junction, keep right. The left-hand track at this junction leads down to **Vault Beach** from where you can regain the coastal path by another track leading uphill. Keep left at the next junction.

Walk 1

③ Go left over a stile and follow a path through scrubland. Keep ahead at a junction signed 'Dodman Point' then go over a stile onto open ground. Continue on this footpath to the summit of Dodman Point.

④ As you approach the large granite cross on the summit of the Dodman, reach a first junction from where a path going right leads to the **Watch House**. Continue towards the cross on the summit and then, just before the cross and at the next junction and arrow post, go right along the coast path.

> **WHAT TO LOOK FOR**
> In Cornwall, 'hedges' generally means granite or slate walls that are bound together with earth and that tend to become dense with mosses and vegetation. All along the damp lanes of the field tracks and on the great embankment of the Bulwark look for common, but colourful plant species which thrive in these conditions. Look for red valerian, with its pink and red flowers, the pink and white dog rose, the violet-coloured selfheal and the cream-coloured honeysuckle.

⑤ Go over a stile beyond a gate with an access notice pinned to it. Reach a junction in a few paces. Turn right and follow the path between the high banks of the **Bulwark**.

> **WHERE TO EAT AND DRINK**
> There are no refreshment places along the route of the walk. The **Old Customs House** licensed café and restaurant in Gorran Haven serves meals all day. Next door is a shop where you can buy ice cream and cakes. The **Haven Café**, further down towards the beach, serves fish and chips to take away. Gorran Haven's pub is the **Llawnroc Inn**. It is reached by walking up Church Street from the entrance to the beach, and then by going left up Chute Lane.

⑥ Keep ahead where a path comes in from the right. Follow the hedged track to reach a kissing gate and a surfaced lane at **Penare**. Turn right along the lane.

⑦ At a junction leave the road and go through a field gate signposted '**Treveague**'. Keep across two fields, then at a road end by houses, turn right, signposted '**Gorran Haven**'. Go left at another signpost and go along a drive behind a house, bearing round right. Go left through a gate and then along a path above a small valley.

⑧ Cross a muddy area by some stepping stones, then go through a gate. Follow the driveway ahead to a T-junction with the public road. Turn right and walk down, with care as there can be traffic, to **Gorran Haven** car park.

> **WHILE YOU'RE THERE**
> Explore **Gorran Haven**, a village with a redoubtable history and with a character that is still intact. Once a busy fishing port engaged in seining for pilchards, the Haven was also visited by larger vessels trading in coal and limestone. Lime for 'sweetening' local fields was extracted from the limestone in a kiln by the beach. Visit the fine little **Chapel of St Just** in Church Street, the restored version of a medieval building that at one time was even used as a fishermen's store.

Tudor Cotehele and Victorian Calstock

A stroll along the River Tamar from Calstock's Victorian viaduct to the Tudor manor house of Cotehele.

Walk 2

•DISTANCE•	4 miles (6.4km)
•MINIMUM TIME•	3hrs
•ASCENT / GRADIENT•	164ft (50m)
•LEVEL OF DIFFICULTY•	
•PATHS•	Excellent woodland tracks, can be muddy in places
•LANDSCAPE•	Wooded riverside
•SUGGESTED MAP•	aqua3 OS Explorer 108 Lower Tamar Valley & Plymouth
•START / FINISH•	Grid reference: SX 436683
•DOG FRIENDLINESS•	Dogs should be kept under control in Cotehele environs
•PARKING•	Calstock Quay car park. Bear right at junction at bottom of steep descent into the village. Free car park, but limited spaces. Often full by mid-morning
•PUBLIC TOILETS•	Calstock Quay, Cotehele House, Cotehele Quay

BACKGROUND TO THE WALK

The River Tamar seems to take its ease at Calstock and Cotehele, where it coils lazily through the lush countryside of the Devon-Cornwall border. Today all is rural peace and quiet. Yet a century ago Calstock was a bustling river port, and had been since Saxon times. Victorian copper and tin mining turned Calstock into an even busier port at which all manner of trades developed, including shipbuilding.

The coming of the railway brought an end to Calstock's importance. The mighty rail viaduct of 1906 that spans the river here is an enduring memorial to progress and to later decline, yet the Calstock of today retains the compact charm of its steep riverside location. The viaduct was built from specially cast concrete blocks – 11,000 of them were made on the Devon shore – and it is a tribute to its design that such thoroughly industrial architecture should seem so elegant today and should have become such an acceptable element in the Tamar scene.

Cotehele

The area's finest architectural gem is the Tudor manor house of Cotehele, the focus of this walk. Cotehele dates mainly from the late 15th and early 16th centuries. In the 17th century the Edgcumbe family, who owned the estate, transferred their seat to Mount Edgcumbe House overlooking Plymouth Sound. Cotehele ceased to be the family's main home and the house was spared too much overt modernisation. Soon the Edgcumbe's came to appreciate the value of the house's Tudor integrity and Cotehele seems to have been preserved for its own sake, from the 18th century onwards.

The Edgcumbe's gave the house to the National Trust in 1947 and Cotehele survives as one of the finest Tudor buildings in England. The medieval plan of the house is intact; the fascinating complex of rooms, unlit by artificial light, creates an authentic atmosphere that transcends any suggestion of 'theme park' history. This is a real insight into how wealthier people lived in Tudor Cornwall. Cotehele was built with privacy and even defence in mind and the materials used are splendidly rustic; the exterior facades have a rough patina that adds to the authenticity.

The Danescombe Valley

The early part of the walk leads beneath an arch of the Calstock Viaduct and on along the banks of the river, past residential properties where busy quays and shipbuilding yards once stood. Most of the walk leads through the deeply wooded Danescombe Valley, whose trees crowd round Cotehele in a seamless merging with the splendid estate gardens. The gardens support azaleas and rhododendrons and a profusion of broadleaf trees, the whole interspersed with terraces and such charming features as a lily pond, a medieval dovecote and a Victorian summerhouse. Below the house, at Cotehele Quay, the preserved sailing barge, the *Shamrock*, and the National Maritime Museum's exhibition rooms, commemorate the great days of Tamar trade. As you walk back to Calstock, along an old carriageway and through the deeper recesses of the Danescombe Valley, it is easy to imagine the remote, yet vibrant life of this once great estate and of the busy river that gave it substance.

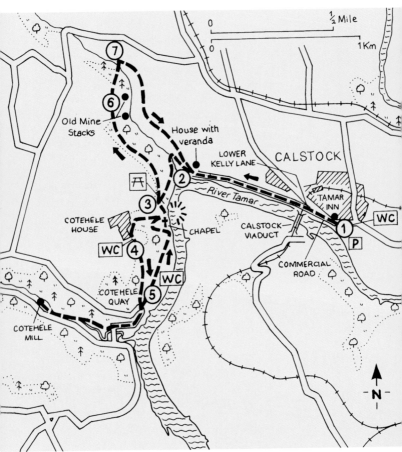

Walk 2 Directions

① From the car park walk to the left of the **Tamar Inn**, then turn left into **Commercial Road**. In a few paces take the second turning left and go along **Lower Kelly Lane** and beneath **Calstock Viaduct**.

② Keep left at a fork just past the large house with a veranda. Beyond a row of cottages, branch left, signposted '**Cotehele House**', and follow a broad track uphill and beneath trees.

WHERE TO EAT AND DRINK

The **Barn Restaurant** is an elegant National Trust restaurant within the Cotehele House complex. It serves morning coffee, afternoon tea and meals using much local produce and has a fine wine list. The **Edgcumbe Arms Tea Room** is an attractive small restaurant at Cotehele Quay offering similar fare to the Barn Restaurant. The **Tamar Inn** at Calstock Quay is right by the start of the walk and is a traditional pub serving a range of bar meals.

③ Go right at a junction, signposted '**Cotehele House**'. Pass above a dovecote in **Cotehele Gardens**, then turn left at a T-junction. Go through a gate and turn right for the entrance to Cotehele House.

④ Follow the road from **Cotehele House**, then branch left and downhill to reach **Cotehele Quay**. (You can continue from the Quay for just under ½ mile (800m) to visit **Cotehele Mill**.)

WHILE YOU'RE THERE

Visit the outstation of the **National Maritime Museum** at Cotehele Quay where the story of Tamar River trade throughout the centuries is told in old pictures and displays. **Cotehele Quay Gallery** has exhibitions of painting and is located by the quay car park. **Cotehele Mill** lies a short distance (signposted) from Cotehele Quay and has been restored to working order.

⑤ Follow a path that starts beside the car park and just beyond **Cotehele Quay Gallery**. Pass a little chapel and then a superb viewpoint to Calstock. At a junction, go right, signposted **Calstock**. In a few paces branch left up a rising track.

⑥ Go right at a junction and descend to a wooden footbridge over a stream. At a T-junction with another track, turn left and walk up the track for about 55 yds (50m).

⑦ Turn sharply right and go up a rising track along the side of a stone wall. Pass a stone pillar and an old well on your left, then pass a junction with a track coming in from the left.

⑧ Join the surfaced lane just before the big house with a veranda, passed earlier. Retrace your steps to **Calstock Quay**.

WHAT TO LOOK FOR

The deep oak and beech woods that cloak the Danescombe Valley and Cotehele are a haven to wild life. The otter, an endangered species, may still be found along the Tamar's banks and although you would be immensely lucky to spot one, keep your eyes peeled. Buzzards lord it above clearings in the trees and above the neighbouring meadows. Along the minor streams, kingfishers, patrol their territory, although again you need to keep a sharp lookout for them. In spring and early summer, the woods and meadows round Cotehele are thick with daffodils and bluebells.

The Vicar of Morwenstow's Gothic World

A walk through Cornwall's most northerly parish, one time home of the eccentric Victorian parson-poet, Robert Stephen Hawker.

•DISTANCE•	7 miles (11.3km)
•MINIMUM TIME•	4hrs
•ASCENT / GRADIENT•	1,640ft (500m) ▲▲ ▲▲ ▲
•LEVEL OF DIFFICULTY•	🚶 🚶 🚶
•PATHS•	Generally good, but inland paths and tracks can be very muddy during wet weather
•LANDSCAPE•	High cliffs punctuated by deep grassy valleys and backed by quiet woods and farmland
•SUGGESTED MAP•	aqua3 OS Explorer 126 Clovelly & Hartland
•START / FINISH•	Grid reference: SS 206154
•DOG FRIENDLINESS•	Dogs off lead in places, but under strict control in fields and grazed cliffland
•PARKING•	Morwenstow: Follow signposted road from the A39 about 2½ miles (4.4km) north of Kilkhampton. Small free car park by Morwenstow Church and Rectory Farm Tearooms
•PUBLIC TOILETS•	Duckpool

BACKGROUND TO THE WALK

The Gothic landscape of North Cornwall's Morwenstow parish, all gaunt sea cliffs, backed by remote farmland and wonderfully gloomy woods, was the ideal environment for the 19th-century parson-poet the Reverend Robert Stephen Hawker. Hawker was vicar of the parish from 1834 to 1874. He was devoted to his parishioners, most of whom were poor farmers and labourers. He cared also for the victims of shipwrecks on the savage Morwenstow coast. There were few survivors, but Hawker made it his duty to bury the dead. He would search the barely accessible foreshore beneath the cliffs, dressed in sea boots and a fisherman's smock, and salvage the often gruesome remains. Legend says that the vicar often dosed his reluctant helpers with gin to overcome their revulsion and superstition. The graveyard at Morwenstow pays homage to the drowned of numerous wrecks.

Hawker is said to have dosed himself with other substances too. He smoked opium, in keeping with the habits of fashionable Romantic poets such as Coleridge and de Quincy. At the tiny 'Hawker's Hut', a driftwood shack that nestles just below the cliff top near the beginning of this walk, he wrote and meditated, often under the influence. He is said to have dressed as a mermaid on occasions, took his pet pig, Gyp, for long walks, and once excommunicated a cat for catching a mouse on Sunday. And why not?

Dramatic Landscape

Take the spirits of Parson Hawker and Gyp the pig with you through this dramatic landscape as you walk from the splendid Church of St Morwenna out to the edge of the great cliffs, to Hawker's Hut. From here the coast path dips into and out of dramatic valleys, often within sight of the slate-grey fins of smooth slabby rock that protrude from the cliff edge. The route leads past the Government's eerie radio tracking station at Cleve where huge satellite receivers cup their ears to the sky.

At Duckpool, the cliffs relent and you turn inland and away from the often boisterous coast to find picturesque thatched cottages beside a placid river ford. Beyond lies the calm of deep woodland. Yet there lingers even here, a sense of Morwenstow's other-worldliness, as the route winds through lonely fields and past handsome old manor houses at Eastaway, Stanbury and Tonacombe to reach Morwenstow's welcoming pub and then Parson Hawker's handsome church once more.

Walk 3

Walk 3 Directions

① Follow the signposted track from the car park to the coast path, then turn left. You'll reach **Hawker's Hut** in about 100yds (91m). Continue from here along the coast path to **Duckpool**.

② When you reach the inlet of Duckpool walk up the road along the bottom of the valley to a T-junction and turn left. At a junction, go right to cross a bridge beside a ford. Follow the lane round left for about 150yds (137m), then bear off left along a broad track through some woodland.

Walk 3

③ Cross a stile on the left, go over a wooden footbridge, climb the slope, then turn right and up a track. Turn left at a T-junction, keep ahead at the next junction, then in 40yds (37m) go right through a metal gate.

④ Follow a field track leading to a surfaced lane at **Woodford**. Turn left and go downhill past **Shears Farm** then round right and uphill to a junction with a road. Turn left past a **bus shelter**.

> **WHAT TO LOOK FOR**
> Parson Hawker's eccentricity extended to the vicarage he built next to Morwenstow church. The house's chimneys replicate the towers of other North Cornwall churches and the tower of an Oxford college. The kitchen chimney is a replica of the tombstone of Hawker's mother.

⑤ Turn left along a path between cottages to a kissing gate. Turn right and then immediately left and follow the edge of the field to a stile on the left. Cross this stile, then cross the next field, bearing slightly left, to reach the hedge on the opposite side.

⑥ Go over two stiles and then straight up the next field, often muddy, to a hedge corner. Go alongside a wall to a hedged track and on to a junction with a surfaced lane.

⑦ Go through a gate opposite, then turn right through a gap. Go left to a stile. Bear left across the next field to its far left-hand corner, then go up to **Stanbury House**. Turn right to reach a surfaced lane.

> **WHILE YOU'RE THERE**
> Morwenstow's **Church of St Morwenna** is unavoidable and unmissable, from its atmospheric graveyard and splendid Norman doorways to its wonderfully gloomy interior. Even the approach to the lychgate has drama. You tread on visible depressions, bare of pebbles, the graves of unsanctified suicides or criminals. Just inside the gate, on the right is a granite cross with the initials of Hawker's wife. The cross on the left commemorates drowned sailors.

⑧ Go left along the lane for a few paces and then over a narrow stile on the right. Go straight across the next two fields to reach a stile and gate into a farm lane behind **Tonacombe House**.

⑨ Go right for a few paces then bear off left along a muddy track. Cross two fields then descend into a wooded valley. Keep right, cross a stream, then go right and up steeply to a stile.

⑩ Cross over the fields to reach a meadow behind the **Bush Inn**. Go down the left side of the buildings, and then up to the road. Turn left for **Morwenstow Church** and the car park.

> **WHERE TO EAT AND DRINK**
> There are no refreshments along the way but the **Bush Inn** is just along the road from Morwenstow Church. It does bar meals and you can enjoy smoked mackerel or crab salad with your Hick's Special Draught. The delightful **Rectory Farm Tearooms & Restaurant** is right at the start of the walk and offers morning coffee, lunches, cream teas and evening meals by arrangement.

Picturesque Broadhembury

Beech woods and rolling farmland around an unspoilt thatched village.

•DISTANCE•	5½ miles (9km)
•MINIMUM TIME•	2hrs 30min
•ASCENT / GRADIENT•	360ft (110m) ▲ ▲ ▲
•LEVEL OF DIFFICULTY•	🚶 🚶 🚶
•PATHS•	Country lanes, pastures and woodland paths, 7 stiles
•LANDSCAPE•	Rolling farmland and beech woods
•SUGGESTED MAP•	aqua3 OS Explorer 115 Exeter & Sidmouth
•START / FINISH•	Grid reference: SY 095068
•DOG FRIENDLINESS•	Possibility of livestock in some fields
•PARKING•	Unsurfaced car park at Knowles Wood
•PUBLIC TOILETS•	By the Drewe Arms in centre of Broadhembury

BACKGROUND TO THE WALK

Broadhembury is one of those unspoilt showpiece Devon villages that gives you the impression that nothing has changed for centuries and that you've entered some sort of time warp. The picturesque main street is lined with well-preserved cob and thatched cottages and pretty flower-filled gardens, and there appears to be a constant cycle of repair and renovation going on. Much of Broadhembury as you see it today developed as an estate village under the patronage of the Drewe family in the early 17th century, and you still get the feeling that this is certainly not a village struggling for survival.

The Drewe Family

St Andrew's Church holds many memorials to members of the family, who have been highly influential in the development of the village. In 1603 Edward Drewe, Sergeant-at-Law to Queen Elizabeth I, bought Abbey Farm from Dunkeswell Abbey, and created a new mansion, The Grange, which remained the family seat for nearly 300 years. Edward Drewe was a successful lawyer, who already owned Sharpham and Killerton. The oak drawing room at The Grange is said to be one of the most beautiful in the country. The house is not open to the public, but you can get a good view of it from the south east approach road to the village.

The church was consecrated in 1259, but the building dates mainly from the 15th century, constructed of local flint and chalky limestone from Beer. It's set at the end of a cul-de-sac of chestnut trees and has been much restored over the last couple of centuries. The tower (from about 1480) is almost 100ft (30m) high. The timbers of the roof were painted in the late 15th century and were only discovered in 1930 when repair work was being carried out. There is also an unusual 15th-century font which is somewhat damaged (probably during the Civil War) and decorated with primitive figures of apostles and clergy, and an 18th-century memorial to Augustus Toplady, who wrote the hymn *Rock of Ages*.

Just a mile (1.6km) to the south east of the village lies Hembury hillfort, on a spur of the Blackdown Hills at 883ft (269m) above sea level. There was a causewayed camp here around 2500 BC, and in about 150 BC Iron Age dwellers built the defensive earthworks that can be seen today. The site was inhabited until around AD 75. The best time of year to explore the hillfort is in May, when the ramparts are smothered with a carpet of bluebells.

Walk 4

Blackborough

Newcombe Common

PONCHYDOWN

Newcombe Common

½ Mile

½ Km

WOODLAND TRUST LAND

Forest Glade House

Knowles Wood

Downlands Plantations

Knowles House

① ▲ 283

North Hill

② Rifle Range

⑧

DEVON & SOMERSET GLIDING CLUB

BARLEYCOMBE FARM

③

Moor Copse

Hanger Farm

⑦

④

R. Tale

Skinners Copse

–N–

⑥

WC

THE DREWE ARMS

Broadhembury ⑤

ST ANDREWS CHURCH

Walk 4 Directions

① Return to the road and turn left uphill. Very shortly a bridleway sign points right through another parking area. After a few minutes this narrow, level path reaches a signpost and metal gate (left), indicating that you have reached the Devon & Somerset Gliding Club. Ignore the gate, continue on the bridleway.

② Pass through the next metal gate onto the airfield. Turn right along the edge, keeping to the right of the clubhouse. Follow the tarmac drive left over a cattle grid and down the lane to join a road.

WHAT TO LOOK FOR ⓘ

The **Devon & Somerset Gliding Club** is near the start of the walk at Northill, over 900ft (280m) above sea level – a popular spot with skylarks, too! The return leg skirts along the edge of the airfield; the gliders are launched using a steel cable, so it's wise to keep well out of the way. There's something quite magical – and tempting – about watching the gliders drift silently through the air above you, often reaching heights of over 2,000ft (600m).

---

③ Turn right; pass **Barleycombe Farm** (on the left), then follow bridleway signs right through a gate, left through another and into a field. Follow the track along the bottom of the field. The path curves right through a stand of beech trees and a metal gate, then runs straight across the next field towards a big beech tree and gate. Take the stony track through the gate. After 100yds (91m) bear right along a grassy path (ignore the gate straight ahead) and through two metal gates, with a coniferous plantation to the right.

④ The path ends at a lane; turn right downhill into **Broadhembury**. At **St Andrew's Church** cross the road and go through the churchyard, then under the lychgate and downhill to find the **Drewe Arms** (left) for a welcome break.

⑤ To continue the walk, from the pub, turn left down the main street to reach the bridge and ford. Turn right up the lane, past the playground and up the hill.

⑥ Just past two thatched cottages go left over the stile in the hedge and up the field, aiming for a stile in the top left corner. Go over that and straight ahead, keeping the old farmhouse and barn conversions to your right. Over the next stile; then another; then right, round the edge of the field, and over a small stile ahead into a small copse. Another stile leads into the next field; look straight across to locate the next stile in the beech hedge opposite, which takes you into a green lane.

⑦ Turn right and walk uphill between conifers, on the left, and fields until a metal gate leads on to an open gateway and back on to the airfield.

⑧ Turn left along the edge of the field. Go left over the second iron gate to rejoin the bridleway which leads back to the road. Turn left downhill to find your car.

WHILE YOU'RE THERE ⓘ

Visit **Broadhembury Craft Centre**, which you will pass as you walk downhill towards the village after Point ④. Open seven days a week and situated in an attractive courtyard setting, here you will find a range of rural craft workshops, as well as the **Corner Café**, serving tea, coffee and light snacks.

Walk 5

The Bampton Notts

Stories from a little-known corner of North East Devon.

•DISTANCE•	5½ miles (9km)
•MINIMUM TIME•	2hrs 30min
•ASCENT / GRADIENT•	425ft (130m) ▲▲▲
•LEVEL OF DIFFICULTY•	林林 林林 林林
•PATHS•	Rough fields, tracks and lanes, 11 stiles
•LANDSCAPE•	Rolling hills and wooded combes
•SUGGESTED MAP•	aqua3 OS Explorer 114 Exeter & the Exe Valley
•START / FINISH•	Grid reference: SX 956223
•DOG FRIENDLINESS•	Not suitable for dogs due to several difficult stiles
•PARKING•	Station Road car park by church in centre of Bampton
•PUBLIC TOILETS•	By car park

BACKGROUND TO THE WALK

Bampton is one of those places that isn't really on the way to anywhere. As you drive north towards Exmoor from Tiverton you might sweep past the turning to Bampton, making for Dulverton up the Barle Valley. But it would be a mistake not to go and have a look at this quiet, ancient town, situated at a natural crossing place on the River Batherm, and whose Saxon origins are still evident in the layout of its building plots, streets and almost circular churchyard. In 1258 a royal charter established St Luke's Fair, one of the oldest in the country, which became famous for the October sale of Exmoor ponies in the late 19th century, and which survives today as a funfair and street market. It's an unspoilt town where the tradition of taking your Christmas Day turkey to the bakery to be cooked still carries on.

An Agricultural Community

Bampton held important cattle and wool sheep markets from the 14th century, and the various fine buildings in the town to be seen today are evidence of wealthier times in the 17th and 18th centuries, when the cloth industry was at its most prosperous. The town was famous for the Bampton Notts, said to be the finest breed of sheep in Devon, but which died out in the late 19th century. Before the coming of the railway in 1884 the sheep were herded on foot to Bristol, 60 miles (197km) away, for sale.

It's worth deviating from your route a little to have a look at the church of St Michael and All Angels in Bampton, dating in part from the 12th century, though an earlier one occupied the site. A late Saxon or early Norman window arch can be seen high in the south wall. An interesting feature here is the stone casing around two enormous yew trees in the churchyard, to prevent the sheep that used to graze here from being poisoned. The roots of these huge trees may be responsible for the cracks that have appeared in the south wall.

As the walk penetrates deeper into the Devon countryside, it reaches the tiny village of Morebath, essentially a farming community, as it has been since Saxon times. It has a remote, yet safe, feel about it. There are warm springs of chalybeate water here in a marshy basin, from which the name Morebath derives. The simple tower of St George's Church probably dates from the 11th century but its most unusual feature is the saddleback roof, part of the 19th-century restoration, which is unlike anything seen elsewhere in the county.

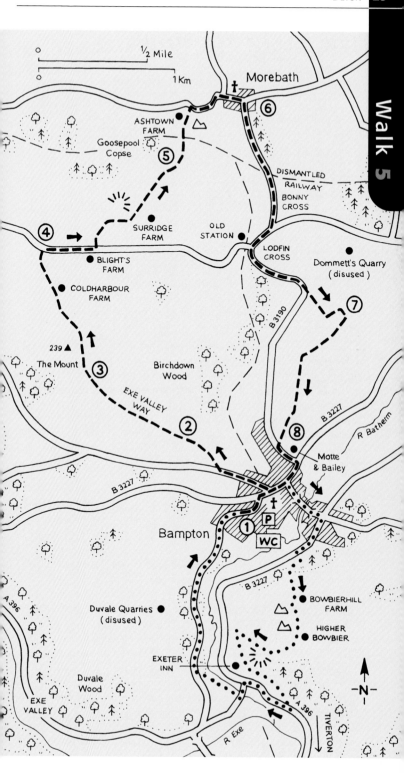

Walk 5

Walk 5 **Directions**

① Leave the car park by the toilets, cross the road and turn left up the steep, narrow lane signposted 'Dulverton'. After a few minutes follow **Exe Valley Way** (EVW) signs right up a drive, left through a gate and up the field keeping right. Cross over the stile and go left on the track to reach a double stile in the top corner of the field. Over that, turn immediately right over another then turn left through a bank of trees and right, uphill (keeping the trees right).

② Follow EVW signs over the next stile, straight across the field to another stile (top left) and left around the field to an open gateway. Turn left, then immediately right, keeping the hedge on your left to reach a metal gate at the hilltop, with views towards Exmoor.

WHERE TO EAT AND DRINK ⓘ

Try the characterful 200-year-old **Seahorse**, a real ale pub on Briton Street at the other end of the town from the car park. The **Jasmine Tearooms**, in the main street, is a great place to go for tea or coffee and a delicious snack.

---

③ Continue downhill through open fields and three gates to reach **Coldharbour Farm**. Follow footpath signs left before the farmhouse then straight ahead on a grassy track, through a gate and downhill to reach the lane through another gate.

④ The EVW goes left here but we turn right up the lane to reach **Blight's Farm** (right). Turn left through a gate and up the track to **Surridge Farm**. Turn left through a big metal gate, then another at the

hilltop, continuing downhill through another gate onto a green lane (muddy in winter). There are views of **Morebath** ahead.

⑤ The lane joins a flinty track; turn left and over the dismantled railway towards **Ashtown Farm** then right down the drive under ancient lime trees. Turn right and follow the deep lane uphill past the **Old Vicarage** to the centre of Morebath.

⑥ Turn right down the B3190, taking care (there's no pavement). At **Bonny Cross** go right (signed 'Bampton') to pass **Lodfin Cross** and the old station. When the road bends sharply right take the stony track straight ahead, slightly uphill.

⑦ At the hilltop a footpath sign leads right over a stile. Go down the field, over a stile then straight on, over a stile and through a gate at the top of the next field. Turn immediately left through another gate. Cross the field diagonally towards the left-hand gate at the top. Pass through the next two fields to a stile in the hedge at the top, then down a narrow fenced path towards **Bampton**. Cross over the next stile and field to gain the road over another stile.

⑧ Turn left, then cross over to take the old road into the town. Turn right and go straight ahead towards the church and your car.

WHAT TO LOOK FOR ⓘ

Beyond Point ⑦ of the walk you get your first sight of the Norman motte and bailey of **Bampton Castle** which was built on Saxon foundations in 1067. Traces of the original enclosure are still visible within the bailey, and Saxon strip system fields can still just be detected to the north east of the mound.

Walk 6

Pinkery Pond to Moles Chamber

Experience quintessential Exmoor among the barrows and tumuli of its Bronze-Age farmers.

•DISTANCE•	5¾ miles (9.2km)
•MINIMUM TIME•	3hrs
•ASCENT / GRADIENT•	700ft (210m) ▲ ▲ ▲
•LEVEL OF DIFFICULTY•	🚶 🚶 🚶
•PATHS•	Narrow moorland paths following fences and some tracks, 4 stiles
•LANDSCAPE•	Bleak, grassy moorland
•SUGGESTED MAP•	aqua3 OS Outdoor Leisure 9 Exmoor
•START / FINISH•	Grid reference: SS 728401
•DOG FRIENDLINESS•	Be aware of possible livestock, ponies and deer on open moorland
•PARKING•	Unmarked roadside pull-off on B3358 on Chains Hill
•PUBLIC TOILETS•	None on route; nearest in Simonsbath car park

BACKGROUND TO THE WALK

Chains Barrow is the highest point on the waterlogged Exmoor plateau of purple moor grass and deer sedge. Other walks hereabouts are Exmoor more or less; this one is Exmoor pure and simple. It has views out to the sea and to the sheltered lands below. It's a walk for a sunny day with skylarks, or for a chill one in autumn. In cloud and rain, with the bog at full squelch, you absorb a lot of atmosphere (and quite a bit of the rain), though this may not be everyone's idea of fun.

Bronze Age Exmoor

In about 2000 BC the hunter-gatherer lifestyle of the Stone Age came to an end on Exmoor. In the Bronze Age that followed we find traces of agriculture, with crops, such as barley, and livestock (mostly cattle and sheep). We also find the round barrows, for example, Chains Barrow and Longstone Barrow, scattered across the moorland summits. Elsewhere in Somerset the standing stones are of the Bronze Age – charred wood accidentally buried under the stones can be carbon-dated. More doubtfully, Tarr Steps in the south of Exmoor are also credited to the Bronze-Age people.

It used to be thought that the change from the Stone Age to the Bronze Age came about by conquest: better swords and axes allowed the new people to kill or enslave the old. Today, tree pollen preserved in peat bogs can be dated very accurately, and shows that the clearance of the moors for farming was a gradual process. The scratch-plough was perhaps more important than the sword: experts believe that it was the idea of sitting still and starting a farm that conquered, rather than a particular tribe. The climate was warmer and drier in those days, and the moorland was grass rather than peat. Large areas will have been hedged and banked for pasture: on Dartmoor, 25,000 acres (10,000ha) of Bronze Age-enclosures have been mapped out.

High Society

The shepherds belonged to a wider social unit than the family or farmstead. At least some of the people in charge had enough importance to build up collections of 50 or 60 axe heads, implying that the Bronze Age farmers weren't entirely peaceful people. Someone else had enough spare time to build the long barrows and raise the standing stones, and there were jewellers working in jadeite and bronze.

It isn't known why the people of the Bronze Age chose to build their barrows here on the bleakest of hilltops. Perhaps they were scared of the spirits of the dead and wanted to keep them out of the way, or perhaps a really large, conspicuous barrow would intimidate the people on the next hill.

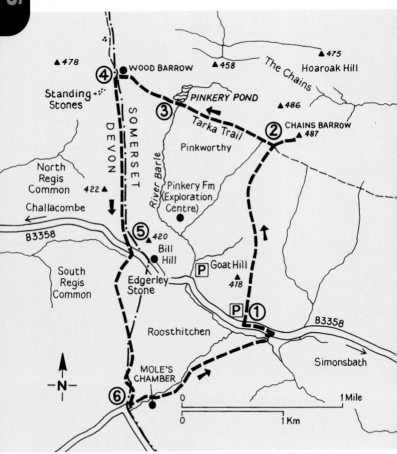

Walk 6 **Directions**

① At the **Simonsbath** end of the pull-off is a gate with a bridleway sign for **Chains Barrow**. Go up the right-hand edges of two fields, then head 35yds (32m) left, to a gate.

The way across the following rough moorland is marked by occasional yellow-topped posts. Go gently uphill, parallel with a hedge away on the left. The marked way bends slightly right, up the crest of a wide moorland spur. At the top is a bank with a gateway.

Walk 6

② A signpost indicates a sketchy path out over the moor to **Chains Barrow**. Return to the gateway and follow the fenced bank. It leads across the moor top to **Pinkery Pond**; this is crossed on its dam.

③ Follow the fence as it continues uphill to a corner of access land. Maintain your direction across moorland for 350yds (320m) to join a high bank, and follow this to the left, to **Wood Barrow**.

> **WHILE YOU'RE THERE** ⓘ
> The **Exmoor Steam Railway** runs steam trains along a mile (1.6km) of narrow gauge track above Bratton Fleming. It's England's highest narrow gauge railway, with wide views over the valley of the Devon Yeo.

④ The gate ahead leads into Devonshire. Beyond, Wood Barrow is one of many put to more conventional use, originally by the Saxons, as markers of the Devon boundary. In front of **Woodbarrow Gate** turn left on a signed bridleway track, with a high bank on its right. This leads off the moor. Bear left around a sheep-pen made of disused metal crash barriers. A gate leads on to the **B3358**.

> **WHAT TO LOOK FOR** ⓘ
> From Wood Barrow, at the top of this walk, the land to the west is an access area under the Country Stewardship Scheme. Here, skilled map readers can go adventuring across the moor in search of **Longstone Barrow**, and the Long Stone itself, a standing stone 9ft (3m) high, raised during the Bronze Age.

⑤ Cross into a track signposted 'Mole's Chamber'. This climbs for ¼ mile (400m) to a signpost. Here you must bear left across featureless moorland for 550yds (503m). A field corner soon comes into sight: on the right is high banking with a fence in front, and on the left is lower banking with a fence on top; between these two is the destination gate. Go straight downhill to a stream, with a peaty track starting beyond it. Follow this up and then bending right, to reach the end of a tarred road.

⑥ Turn left, away from the road. A faint old track runs down across a stream to a narrow gate with a blue paint-spot. An improving path runs down to the right of the stream, gradually slanting up to a gate. Here join a larger track, but immediately after the gate keep ahead as the larger track bends right. A faint green track runs parallel with the river down on the left, to reach a signposted gate. Turn left on a tarred track, to join the **B3358**. Turn left to the parking pull-off.

> **WHERE TO EAT AND DRINK** ⓘ
> The **Exmoor Forest Hotel** at Simonsbath serves good food and Exmoor Ale (brewed in Wiveliscombe), but no lunches in winter. Dogs are welcome. The bar is decorated with bits of dead animals. Indeed, this is your best chance of sighting a badger: there's a stuffed one on the wall above the fireplace.

Walk 7

Quantock Coastline: Kilve and East Quantoxhead

With the risk of French invasion now passed, you can spy out these Tudor villages and breezy cliffs without fearing arrest.

•DISTANCE•	3 miles (4.8km)
•MINIMUM TIME•	1hr 30min
•ASCENT / GRADIENT•	250ft (80m) ▲▲▲
•LEVEL OF DIFFICULTY•	👫 👫 👫
•PATHS•	Tracks, field paths, and grassy cliff top, 7 stiles
•LANDSCAPE•	Tudor villages, farmland and coastline
•SUGGESTED MAP•	aqua3 OS Explorer 140 Quantock Hills & Bridgwater
•START / FINISH•	Grid reference: ST 144442
•DOG FRIENDLINESS•	Extra care along cliff top, unstable near edge
•PARKING•	Pay-and-display at sea end of Sea Lane
•PUBLIC TOILETS•	At car park (closed October – February)

BACKGROUND TO THE WALK

With two Tudor villages, industrial remnants up to only a century ago, and a lucid display of geology underfoot, this is a walk to stimulate the brain as well as the lungs.

Jobs for the Priests

The chantry chapel at Kilve is built in the local grey shale, but with the arches picked out in orange Quantock sandstone. The sandstone is easier to work into shaped blocks, but has been eroded by the sea winds. This chantry housed five priests whose sole function was the saying of prayers and masses for the deceased Simon de Furneaux and his family. The doctrine was that the rich could pay their way out of purgatory by setting up such chapels. This created employment for priests, but contributed to the general loss of credibility of the Catholic faith. In fact Kilve Chantry closed even before the Reformation, when a Lollard dissenter married into the family in the late-14th century. Later it was used by smugglers for storing brandy and burnt down around 1850 in an alcohol fire. Behind the ruins, the Chantry House has a pigeon loft still in use.

The old (possibly Saxon) preaching cross in Quantoxhead churchyard is a viewpoint for the Manor House. It also looks on to the back of Quantoxhead Farm, where the semi-circular wing is a horse-gang. This once housed a capstan where horses walked in circles to power, via an endless belt, farm machinery in the main building. The church itself has fossils incorporated into the walls, and Tudor-carved pew ends.

The Spies who Wrote Sonnets

When Samual Taylor Coleridge and William Wordsworth walked here, their particular interest was in the Holford stream. Coleridge planned a poem in his deceptively simple 'conversational' style, tracing the stream from its birth high in Hodder Combe. However, the two famous Romantic poets had already aroused local suspicions by their comings and goings, and both had been enthusiastic supporters of the French Revolution in its early days. This was 1797: England was in the grip of invasion fever; and Kilve has a small but usable harbour. Accordingly, a government agent called James Walsh was sent to investigate. He quizzed a footman about their dinner-time conversation: it was reported as being quite impossible to understand, which was, of course, most suspicious. The agent followed them to Kilve. Lurking behind a gorse bush, he heard them discussing 'Spy Nosy' and thought he'd been found out. They had actually been talking about the German philosopher, Spinoza… Coleridge never got round to writing his poem *The Brook* – but Wordsworth did. Twenty years later, he adopted his friend's plan into a sequence of sonnets on Lakeland's River Duddon.

Walk 7

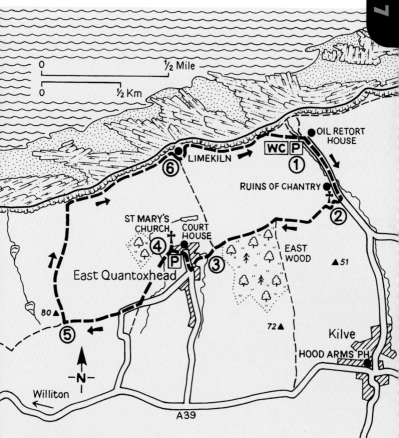

Walk 7 Directions

① From the car park head back along the lane to the ruined chantry. Turn into the churchyard through a lychgate. Such gates were built to shelter coffins and their bearers: this one is too small for its

purpose, so must be a modern reconstruction. Pass to the left of the church, to a kissing gate.

② A signposted track crosses a field to a gate with a stile; bear right to another gate with a stile and pass along the foot of **East Wood**. (At its far end, a stile allows wandering

Walk 7

into the wood, from April to August
only.) Ignoring the stile on the left,
keep ahead to a field gate with a
stile and a track crossing a stream.

③ The track bends left past gardens
and ponds of **East Quantoxhead** to
reach a tarred lane. Turn right,
towards the Tudor **Court House**,
but before its gateway bear left into
a car park. Pass through to a tarred
path beyond two kissing gates. In
an open field this bears right, to
St Mary's Church.

④ Return to the first kissing gate
but don't go through, instead
bearing right to a field gate, and
crossing the field beyond to a lane.
Turn right and, where the lane
bends left, keep ahead into a green
track. At its top, turn right at a
'Permissive path' noticeboard.

⑤ Follow field edges down to the
cliff top, and turn right. A clifftop
path leads to a stile before a sharp

dip, with a ruined limekiln
opposite. This was built around
1770 to process limestone shipped
from Wales into lime for the fields
and for mortar. Most of the rest of
Somerset is limestone, but it was
still easier to bring it by sea across
the Bristol Channel.

⑥ Turn around the head of the dip,
and back left to the cliff top. Here
an iron ladder descends to the
foreshore: you can see alternating
layers of blue-grey lias (a type of
limestone) and grey shale. Fossils
can be found here, but be aware
that the cliffs are unstable – hard
hats are now standard wear for
geologists. Alternatively, given a
suitably trained dog and the right
sort of spear, you could pursue the
traditional sport of 'glatting' –
hunting conger eels in the rock
pools. Continue along the wide
clifftop path until a tarred path
bears off to the right, crossing the
stream studied by Coleridge, into
the car park.

The White Horse at Osmington

Where the world saw a sane King George III take a well-earned break.

•DISTANCE•	4 miles (6.4km)
•MINIMUM TIME•	2hrs
•ASCENT / GRADIENT•	568ft (173m) ▲ ▲ ▲
•LEVEL OF DIFFICULTY•	🚶 🚶 🚶
•PATHS•	Farm and village lanes, woodland paths, field paths, 9 stiles
•LANDSCAPE•	Sheltered green valley behind coastline and chalky ridge of White Horse Hill
•SUGGESTED MAP•	aqua3 OS Explorer OL 15 Purbeck & South Dorset
•START / FINISH•	Grid reference: SY 724829
•DOG FRIENDLINESS•	No problems
•PARKING•	Church Lane in Osmington, just off A353
•PUBLIC TOILETS•	None on route

BACKGROUND TO THE WALK

The 1994 film *The Madness of King George* did much to remind the world of a monarch whose identity had been obscured by time. In the Dorset town of Weymouth, however, he has never been forgotten.

Weymouth is a trading port with a patchy history, including the first outbreak on English shores of the Black Death and a proximity to France that had left it vulnerable to raids. The town found new life in the 18th century as a base for trade with the Americas and the shipping of convicts to Australia. The 1780s saw the emergence of the popular cult of sea bathing (and even seawater drinking) – Weymouth joined in. A royal visit in 1789, however, was to rocket the little town into the top rank of seaside resorts.

Holiday Spin

Rumours of George III's mental instability were threatening to destabilise the country. Accordingly, it was decided that the King should go on a short and highly visible tour, to enable his subjects to see how much better he was. Weymouth was picked, and a six-day journey commenced for the royal party, which consisted of the King, the Queen and the three princesses. It was a great build-up and, by the time they reached Weymouth, the crowds were ecstatic, with bunting, mayoral receptions and gunships firing salutes in the bay. The King responded to their warmth with a short walk-about on his very first evening and the declaration that he 'never saw a sight so pleasing'.

Patriotic Band

Any hopes that the King might have had of a quiet dip in the sea, however, were dashed a week later by the strength and volume of local enthusiasm for their royal visitor. Even as his royal-crested bathing hut was being wheeled into the sea, a band hidden in a nearby bathing machine were waiting to burst into a loyal song as soon as the regal body hit the water. George III spent ten weeks here on his first visit, enjoying day trips to Lulworth, Milton

Abbey and St Adhelm's Head, and sailing off Portland. The royal family returned two years later for a holiday and then returned every year until 1805.

In 1808 John Rainier (brother of the heroic Rear Admiral Peter Rainier, whose name was given to Mount Rainier near Seattle), arranged for a symbol of the town's undying loyalty and gratitude for the royal attention bestowed upon them, to be carved into the chalk downs above Osmington. And so an elegant silhouette of the King on horseback was created, around 324ft (99m) high, riding away from the town – presumably in a much healthier condition after his vacation. Once clearly visible from Weymouth, Portland and ships out at sea, today the chalk figure is weathered and grey, but you can still pick out the graceful lines of the horse's legs and tail, and the King's distinctive cocked hat.

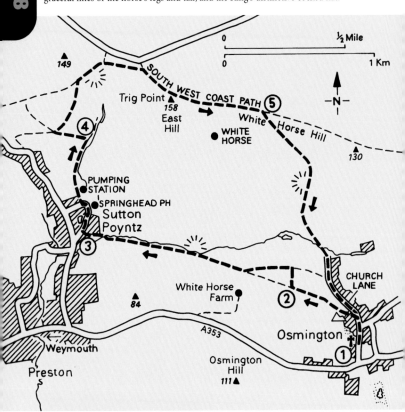

Walk 8 Directions

① From **Osmington church** walk down the village street of pretty thatched cottages. At the junction keep on down **Church Lane**. Opposite **Forge Barn**, at the end of a wall, turn left up a long, steep flight of steps, signed 'Sutton Poyntz'. The path rises through

woodland. After a second set of steps bear right on the path which undulates through the trees. Cross a stile and continue straight on to the end of a field.

② Cross a stile and turn immediately right to cross a second stile and walk down the field. Turn left through a gate and head straight across the field. Cross a

Walk 8

farm track and bear ahead and right. Cross a pair of stiles and continue along the bottom of the field, looking to your right to see the **White Horse**. Continue though a gap. At the end of the next field bear left, through a gateway, then go straight on (yellow marker), towards **Sutton Poyntz**. Soon veer right, cross a stream and bear left through a gate. Follow the path to a stile and continue to the road.

③ Turn right, pass the **Mill House** and the tall, red brick mill on the left. Pass the village pond and the **Springhead** pub on the right. Bear left and right up a lane by **Springfield Cottage**. Go through a gate and follow the track straight ahead. Go through another gate, with a pumping station on the right, below the bottom of the steep combe where the spring emerges.

④ Cross a stile by a gate and turn left up the grassy lane. About half-way up the hill turn right, up a track (the upper of two) that leads to the top above the combe, with great views along the valley and down to **Weymouth Bay** and **Portland**. Keep right on the green track, go through a gate and keep left along the field edge. Follow the path round to the right and walk up the field (a lane soon joins from the left). Stay on this track past the trig point. Go through a gate and keep straight on, with a good view to strip lynchets on the hillside ahead.

WHAT TO LOOK FOR
As you walk along White Horse Hill there is a clear view of terracing on the grassy slopes of the combe ahead. These are **strip lynchets**, relics of a farming system introduced in the 12th and 13th centuries in Dorset, to maximise the land available for cultivation. There are further good examples of these medieval earthworks in the hills around Worth Matravers.

⑤ Go through a gate and bear down to the right, signed 'Osmington'. The track leads down the hill, through a gate – look back to see the White Horse again. Follow the lane back up through the village to your car.

Walk 9

Horton's Rebel King

A luscious landscape, where once a rebel was roused.

•DISTANCE•	7½ miles (12.1km)
•MINIMUM TIME•	4hrs
•ASCENT / GRADIENT•	426ft (130m) ▲ ▲ ▲
•LEVEL OF DIFFICULTY•	🚶 🚶 🚶
•PATHS•	Field paths, tracks, some road, 15 stiles
•LANDSCAPE•	Gently rolling farmland, mixed woodland
•SUGGESTED MAP•	aqua3 OS Explorer OL 22 New Forest; Explorer 118
•START / FINISH•	Shaftesbury & Cranborne Chase
•DOG FRIENDLINESS•	Grid reference: SU 034072 (on Explorer 118)
	On lead on road sections
•PARKING•	Lay-by with phone box, just west of Horton
•PUBLIC TOILETS•	None on route

BACKGROUND TO THE WALK

The countryside around Horton holds a sad reminder of a flamboyant rebel, who was captured here after being discovered asleep in a ditch below an ash tree. On 11 June 1685 James, Duke of Monmouth, the illegitimate son of the late King Charles II, landed from exile in Holland at Lyme Regis. West Dorset was a base for anti-Catholic Dissenters and on earlier visits the Duke had been warmly greeted with cries of 'God bless the Protestant Duke, and the Devil take the Pope'. He believed he could raise enough support in the West Country to claim the throne from his uncle, the Catholic James II.

Accompanied by a small band of supporters, Monmouth set about recruiting. He announced that he had come to defend the Protestant religion and to deliver the country from the tyranny of James II. Within a few days his following had grown to 4,000. At Taunton Monmouth had himself declared King. On 6 July the rebels clashed with James II's forces at Sedgemoor, across the border in Somerset. The battle was over in 90 minutes, with a loss of 16 of the King's men and some 300 rebels. His ill-equipped army having been routed, the Duke was forced to flee with three followers. He hoped to escape on foot, disguised as a local shepherd, through Dorset to the coast at Poole, where he could board a ship.

However, rewards were posted, and the countryside quickly filled with troops seeking the rebel leader. Two of his companions were caught at Holt the next morning. The Duke and his last companion, a German officer named Buyse, fled across the fields of Horton Heath, but were spotted climbing a hedge by an old lady, Amy Farrant, who told the authorities. Buyse was soon captured and a few hours later militiaman Henry Parkin, while searching beneath an ash tree, discovered another exhausted figure. A search of his pockets disclosed the badge of the Knight of the Garter, golden guineas and recipes for cosmetics, revealing that this was no ordinary shepherd. After a defiant declaration that, given the chance, he would do it all again, Monmouth was taken to London. He was beheaded on 15 July.

The repercussions of the failed rebellion were felt hard in Dorset. The brutal Lord Chief Justice Jeffreys was put in charge of the trials of 312 of Monmouth's supporters in what became known as the 'Bloody Assizes' at Dorchester. Most were transported to the colonies, but 74 were executed, their bodies publicly mutilated and hung on display.

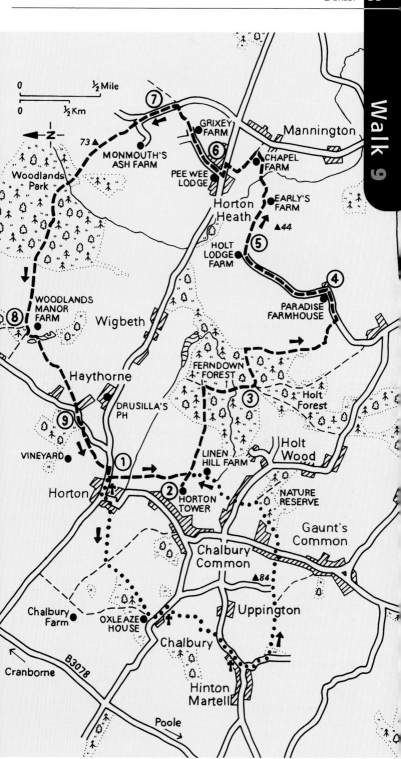

Walk 9

Walk 9 Directions

① Go towards the village and turn left over the stile by the **pump**. Head towards Horton Tower, crossing two more stiles. Go up the hill, bearing diagonally left. Cross the fence at the top corner, and turn right to view the tower.

② Retrace your steps and stay on the track through a gate into **Ferndown Forest.** After ¼ mile (400m) join a firmer track. Shortly, turn right between trees. Cross a stream and a track to a gate.

③ Pass this, go through a bank and turn left along a forest ride. Turn right before the edge of the wood, and follow the path for ¾ mile (1.2km). Bear left at the bottom, down a track. Turn left at the road and pass **Paradise Farmhouse.**

④ Turn left between the houses and follow the road to **Holt Lodge Farm**. With the buildings to your left, bear half-right across the yard to a grassy lane.

⑤ Where this peters out bear left into the field, with the hedge to your right. Cross a stile and go through a gate to **Early's Farm**. Turn immediately left to the gate, and right, in front of the house, into a lane. At a junction after **Chapel Farm**, turn left, signed the 'Long House'. Turn right at the gate and cross a stile. Bear left around the field, cross a stile by a bungalow and another stile to the road.

⑥ Turn left, then right into the lane by **Pee Wee Lodge**. Keep straight on at the junction, then fork right into **Grixey Farm**. Follow the waymarker up the hill, crossing two stiles. With a copse on your left, go up the field. Cross a stile and turn left on to the road.

⑦ After ½ mile (800m) bear left, signed 'Monmouth's Ash Farm', and take the path to the right of the bungalow. Keep straight on this bridleway up over a sandy heath and down into woodland. After a mile (1.6km) the track emerges from the woods, and you can see Horton Tower.

WHERE TO EAT AND DRINK

On the main road east of Horton village is **Drusilla's**, a cosy old pub with a thatched roof, real ales and a fabulous view over to Horton Tower. If you're after a Dorset cream tea, try the **Horton Inn**, at a junction 1 mile (1.6km) west of the village – children and dogs welcome.

---

⑧ Just past **Woodlands Manor Farm** turn left along the road with the fence. Bear down to the right beside the lake and stay on this road. After it becomes a track, look for two stiles in the hedge on the right, just after the farm. Cross these and go diagonally across the field to another stile. Cross the top of the next field and a stile, turning right to meet the road.

⑨ Turn left through **Haythorne** but, before the road descends, go right, through trees, to a gate and down the field, to emerge by the vineyard. Turn left and left again to return to your car.

WHAT TO LOOK FOR

The landmark folly of **Horton Tower** stands like a giant rocket-launcher, splendidly isolated on its hilltop. Some 230ft (70m) high, it was built by Humphrey Sturt in 1762 as an 'observatory', probably for deer-spotting, and was restored in 1994.

Salisbury's Historic Trail

A gentle urban stroll around the streets and ancient pathways of one of England's loveliest Cathedral cities.

•DISTANCE•	3 miles (4.8km)
•MINIMUM TIME•	2hrs (longer if visiting attractions)
•ASCENT / GRADIENT•	Negligible
•LEVEL OF DIFFICULTY•	챯챯
•PATHS•	Pavements and metalled footpaths
•LANDSCAPE•	City streets and water-meadows
•SUGGESTED MAP•	aqua3 OS Explorer 130 Salisbury & Stonehenge; AA Salisbury streetplan
•START / FINISH•	Grid reference: SU 141303
•DOG FRIENDLINESS•	Not suitable for dogs
•PARKING•	Central car park (signed off A36 Ring Road)
•PUBLIC TOILETS•	Central car park, Market Place, Queen Elizabeth Gardens

BACKGROUND TO THE WALK

Salisbury, or New Sarum, founded in 1220 following the abandonment of Old Sarum and built at the confluence of four rivers, is one of the most beautiful cathedral cities in Britain. Relatively free from the sprawling suburbs and high-rise development common in most cities, the surrounding countryside comes in to meet the city streets along the river valleys. Throughout the city centre, buildings of all styles blend harmoniously, from the 13th-century Bishop's Palace in The Close, the medieval gabled houses and historic inns and market places to stately pedimented Georgian houses and even the modern shopping centre. You will discover a host of architectural treasures on this gentle city stroll.

Majestic Cathedral and Close

Salisbury's skyline is dominated by the magnificent spire of the cathedral, which makes a graceful centrepiece to the unified city. An architectural masterpiece, built in just 38 years during the 13th century, the cathedral is unique for its uniformity of style. The tower and spire, with a combined height of 404ft (123m) – the tallest in England – were added in 1334, and the west front of the building is lavishly decorated with row upon row of beautifully carved statues in niches. The rich and spacious interior contains huge graceful columns of Purbeck stone, which line the high-vaulted nave and many windows add to the airy, dignified interior. You will find the impressive tombs and effigies in the nave, the fine cloisters and the library, home to a copy of the Magna Carta, of particular interest.

Originally built to house the clerics, the Cathedral Close is the one of the largest and finest in Britain. It is entered by a series of medieval gateways and contains several grand structures in a rich variety of architectural styles, dating from the 13th century to the present day. Four of these fine buildings are open to the public as museums. The highlights are probably Malmesbury House, originally a 13th-century canonry, with its magnificent roccoco plasterwork and an Orangery that once sheltered Charles II, and Mompesson House (owned by the National Turst), an exquisite Queen Anne building with period furnishings, china and paintings.

Walk 10

City Streets

Beyond The Close, Salisbury is a delight to explore on foot. You can wander through a fascinating network of medieval streets and alleys, lined with half-timbered and jettied houses, enjoying names like Fish Row, Silver Street and Ox Row. On this city walk you will see St Thomas' Church (1238), noted for its 15th-century Doom painting, believed to be the largest painting of the Last Judgment in existence, and pass the hexagonally buttressed 15th-century Poultry Cross, the last of four market crosses in the city. Note, too, the timbered medieval houses, John A'Port and William Russel's (Watsons china shop) in Queen Street, and the Joiners' Hall with its superb Jacobean façade in St Ann Street.

Away from the hustle and bustle, your riverside stroll through Queen Elizabeth's Gardens and along the Town Path to Harnham Mill will reveal the famous view across the water-meadows to the cathedral, much admired by many an artist.

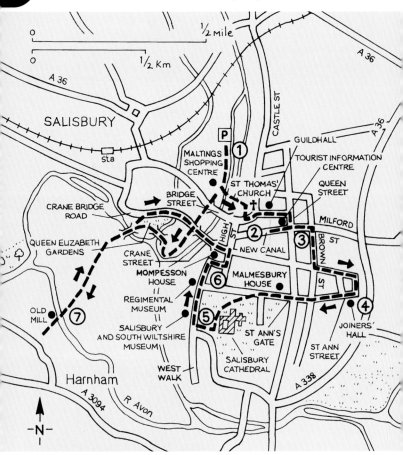

Walk 10 **Directions**

① Join the **Riverside Walk** and follow the path through the **Maltings Shopping Centre**. Keep

beside the Avon tributary stream to reach **St Thomas Square**, close to Michael Snell Tea Rooms and St Thomas' Church. Bear right to the junction of **Bridge Street**, **Silver Street** and the **High Street**.

Walk 10

② Turn left along **Silver Street** and cross the pedestrian crossing by the Haunch of Venison pub to the **Poultry Cross**. Keep ahead along **Butcher Row** and **Fish Row** to pass the Guildhall and tourist information centre. Turn right along **Queen Street** and turn right along **New Canal** to view the cinema foyer.

③ Return to the crossroads and continue ahead along **Milford Street** to pass the Red Lion. Turn right along **Brown Street**, then left along **Trinity Street** to pass Trinity Hospital. Pass Love Lane into **Barnard Street** and follow the road right to reach **St Ann Street**, opposite the Joiners' Hall.

> ### WHERE TO EAT AND DRINK ⓘ
> Old pubs, tea rooms and restaurants abound around the cathedral and its close. Try the excellent **Le Hérisson** café and deli in Crane Street, **Michael Snell Tea Rooms** in St Thomas Square, the historic **Haunch of Venison** in Minster Street, and **Apres LXIX**, a bistro offering modern British food, in New Street. Enjoy a civilised afternoon tea in the garden of **Mompesson House** in The Close.

④ Walk down St Ann Street and keep ahead on merging with Brown Street to reach the T-junction with **St John Street**. Cross straight over and go through St Ann's Gate into the **Cathedral Close**. Pass Malmesbury House and Bishops Walk and take the path diagonally left across the green to reach the main entrance to the cathedral.

> ### WHAT TO LOOK FOR ⓘ
> Go into the foyer of the cinema in New Canal to view John Halle's 15th-century banqueting hall. Composer George Frideric Handel is thought to have given his first concert in England in the room above St Ann Street Gate. While in the cathedral, look out for the 14th-century clock, believed to be the oldest working clock in the world.

⑤ Pass the entrance, walk beside the barrier ahead and turn right. Shortly, turn right again along **West Walk**, passing Salisbury and South Wiltshire Museum, Discover Salisbury (in the Medieval Hall), and the Regimental Museum. Keep ahead into **Chorister Green** to pass Mompesson House.

⑥ Bear left through the gates into **High Street** and turn left at the crossroads along **Crane Street**. Cross the River Avon and turn left along the metalled path beside the river through **Queen Elizabeth Gardens**. Keep left by the play area and soon cross the footbridge to follow the **Town Path** across the water-meadows to the **Old Mill** (hotel) in Harnham.

⑦ Return along Town Path, cross the footbridge and keep ahead to **Crane Bridge Road**. Turn right, recross the Avon and turn immediately left along the riverside path to **Bridge Street**. Cross straight over and follow the path ahead towards **Bishops Mill**. Walk back through the **Maltings Shopping Centre** to the car park.

> ### WHILE YOU'RE THERE ⓘ
> Discover more about Salisbury's fascinating history by visiting the award-winning **Salisbury and South Wiltshire Museum**, housed in the 14th-century King's House within The Close. In the Medieval Hall, also in The Close, **Discover Salisbury** offers a big screen presentation of the city's history and attractions. Climb the steps up the cathedral tower for a bird's-eye view across the city and surrounding countryside.

Avebury – Pagan Pastures

Explore the famous stone circle and some fine prehistoric monuments.

•DISTANCE•	5 miles (8km)
•MINIMUM TIME•	2hrs 30min
•ASCENT / GRADIENT•	262ft (80m) ▲▲ ▲
•LEVEL OF DIFFICULTY•	🚶 🚶 🚶
•PATHS•	Tracks, field paths, some road walking, 3 stiles
•LANDSCAPE•	Downland pasture, water-meadows, woodland and village
•SUGGESTED MAP•	aqua3 OS Explorer 157 Marlborough & Savernake Forest
•START / FINISH•	Grid reference: SU 099696
•DOG FRIENDLINESS•	Keep dogs under control across pasture and NT property
•PARKING•	Large National Trust car park in Avebury
•PUBLIC TOILETS•	Avebury

BACKGROUND TO THE WALK

A vebury's great stone circle is one of the most important megalithic monuments in Europe and it shares it setting with a pretty village. The 200 stones (only 27 remain) were enclosed in a massive earthen rampart nearly a mile (1.6km) in circumference. One can only wonder at the skill, vision and beliefs, not to mention the sheer dogged hard work, which enabled the peoples of that time to move huge stones for many miles and dig thousands of tons of earth to create such landscapes.

Alexander Keiller's Vision

The views presented to today's visitor to Avebury owe as much to archaeologist Alexander Keiller as to the vision of our ancient ancestors. Keiller was the heir to a fortune made from marmalade and was able to indulge in his passion for archaeology. In the early 1930s he came to Avebury, which then had a thriving community within and around the 4,500-year-old circle, and determined to restore it to how it must have looked originally; a prehistoric complex on a scale to match any in the country.

All his energies and a large part of his fortune was spent on purchasing the land, excavating the stones, and although contentious to modern archaeologists, he re-erected fallen stones and set up concrete markers to replace those he believed were missing. Trees were cleared from the ditches and, as and when the opportunity arose, buildings within the circle were purchased and demolished. Some of the villagers left the area and others went to the new houses in nearby Avebury Truslow.

Keiller's work was curtailed by lack of funds and, after the Second World War, he sold the site to the National Trust. His full dreams were never realised and questions were raised as to whether he should have tried to restore the site. Should ancient landscapes be protected by riding roughshod over the interests of those who have subsequently come to live and work there? Whatever your views, there is much to see and enjoy on this walk.

Walking around Avebury is a memorable experience. Unlike Stonehenge, you can roam freely here and this enthralling walk lets you explore some of Britain's finest prehistoric monuments. There is an imposing 1½ mile (2.4km) avenue of standing stones from where, perhaps, ancient processions would lead down to Silbury Hill, an entirely artificial structure

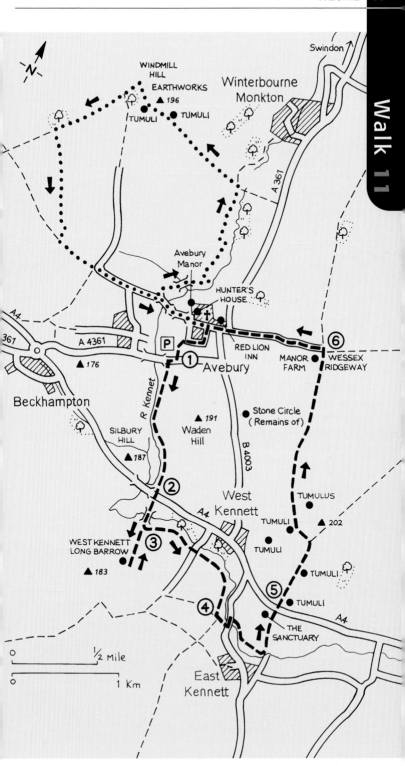

N

Swindon

WINDMILL HILL
EARTHWORKS

Winterbourne Monkton

▲ 196
TUMULI   TUMULI

A 361

Avebury Manor

HUNTER'S HOUSE

A 4

A 361

A 4361

P

▲ 176

① Avebury

RED LION INN

MANOR FARM

WESSEX RIDGEWAY

⑥

Beckhampton

R Kennet

▲ 191
Waden Hill

Stone Circle (Remains of)

B 4003

SILBURY HILL

▲ 187

②

West Kennett

A 4

TUMULUS

TUMULI   ▲ 202

WEST KENNETT LONG BARROW

③

TUMULI

▲ 183

TUMULI

④

⑤

TUMULI

A 4

THE SANCTUARY

½ Mile

1 Km

East Kennett

130ft (40m) high. Smaller in scale but just as thought provoking is the West Kennett Long Barrow, the second largest barrow in Britain at 300ft (91m) in length, and there is a liberal scattering of tumuli over the entire area, the last resting places of many a noble and priest. Finally, alongside the A4 and doubtless unnoticed by many motorists, is The Sanctuary, the site of major wooden buildings, possibly used for religious and burial rites. Or did they, like us, take pleasure from seeking views across our wonderful countryside?

Walk 11 Directions

① From the car park, walk back to the main road and turn right. In 50yds (46m), cross and go through a gate, signed '**West Kennett Long Barrow**'. Pass through another gate and follow the path alongside the **River Kennet**. Go through two more gates and cross two stiles, your route passing **Silbury Hill**.

② Beyond a gate, walk down the right-hand field edge to a gate and the **A4**. Cross straight over and turn left, then almost immediately right through a gate. Walk down the gravel track and cross a bridge over a stream, the track soon narrowing to a footpath. Go through a kissing gate and turn sharp left.

③ To visit **West Kennett Long Barrow** shortly turn right. Otherwise go straight on around the left-hand field edge to a gate and continue along a track. At a staggered junction, keep ahead across a stile and walk along the right-hand field boundary. Keep right in the corner by a redundant stile and cross the stile on your right in the next corner and proceed up a narrow footpath.

④ At a T-junction, turn left and descend to the road. Turn left, then just beyond the bridge, take the bridle path sharp right. Follow the right-hand field edge to a gap in the corner and keep left through the next field. At the top you'll see tumuli right and **The Sanctuary** left. Continue to the **A4**.

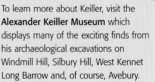

> **WHILE YOU'RE THERE**
> To learn more about Keiller, visit the **Alexander Keiller Museum** which displays many of the exciting finds from his archaeological excavations on Windmill Hill, Silbury Hill, West Kennet Long Barrow and, of course, Avebury.

⑤ Cross the **A4** and head up the **Ridgeway**. After 500yds (457m), turn left off the Ridgeway on to a byway. Bear half-right by the clump of trees on a tumuli and keep to the established track, eventually reaching a T-junction by a series of farm buildings, **Manor Farm**.

⑥ Turn left, signed '**Avebury**', and follow the metalled track through the earthwork and straight over the staggered crossroads by the **Red Lion Inn**. Turn left opposite the National Trust signpost and walk back to the car park.

> **WHAT TO LOOK FOR**
> Wander freely around the **stone circles**, locate the huge Druid Stone, the Swindon Stone and the Barber Stone, and marvel at how they were transported and why they stay upright.

> **WHERE TO EAT AND DRINK**
> Try the thatched **Red Lion** in the heart of the stone circle for traditional pub food and atmosphere. Good home-made vegetarian, mostly organic food and cream teas can be enjoyed at the **Circle Restaurant** off the High Street.

Carisbrooke's Castle

Explore a castle with strong royal associations and visit an isolated church.

•DISTANCE•	6½ miles (10.4km)
•MINIMUM TIME•	2hrs 30min
•ASCENT / GRADIENT•	764ft (233)m ▲▲▲
•LEVEL OF DIFFICULTY•	🚶🚶 🚶🚶 🚶
•PATHS•	Field and downland paths and tracks, some roads, 4 stiles
•LANDSCAPE•	Farmland and open chalk downland
•SUGGESTED MAP•	aqua3 OS Outdoor Leisure 29 Isle of Wight
•START / FINISH•	Grid reference: SZ 489876
•DOG FRIENDLINESS•	Keep dogs under control
•PARKING•	Car park close to Carisbrooke Priory
•PUBLIC TOILETS•	Carisbrooke Castle

BACKGROUND TO THE WALK

You should spend some time discovering the history of Carisbrooke Castle, surely one of the island's finest treasures, before setting out on this downland ramble. On a spur of chalk downland, 150ft (46m) above the village, the site of a Roman fort, this grand medieval ruin commands a perfect military location, overlooking the Bowcombe Valley and the approaches to the heart of the island. You can walk the battlements, experience the majestic location and admire the countryside below, much of the view encompassing the walk ahead.

Norman Strength

The castle is probably of Saxon origin, but it was the Normans who strengthened the site, building the stone walls, the gatehouse and the keep, on a mound within the walls. The outer bastions were built to guard against the 16th-century threat of Spanish invasion. It was said that 'He who held Carisbrooke, held the Isle of Wight.' For centuries the castle went hand-in-hand with the lordship of the island, before the Crown retained the lordship in the 16th century and appointed a Governor of the Island, a title that continues today. The Great Hall, which was the official residence of the Island Governor until 1944, now houses the Isle of Wight Museum. If you visit the Carisbrooke Castle Story in the gatehouse, you'll learn more about the two occasions when it experienced military action, in 1136 and 1377, and find many exhibits about the castle's most famous royal visitor, King Charles I. He sought refuge here during the Civil War in November 1647, but was imprisoned by the Governor until September 1648 before being taken to London for trial and execution. He made two unsuccessful attempts to escape, one from the north curtain wall near the postern gate. You can see the window (a plaque marks the spot) where the King had cut the bars before he was thwarted. His children, the future Charles II, Henry, Duke of Gloucester, and 14 year-old Elizabeth (who died of pneumonia) were also detained here in 1650.

Leaving the castle, the walk takes you through the peaceful Bowcombe Valley, beside the Lukely Brook, to the isolated village of Gatcombe, nestling in a valley between rolling downland. Quarries here provided stone for the building of Carisbrooke Castle. Each stone, it is said, was passed along a human chain to the site 2 miles (3.2km) away. Take a little time to explore the 13th-century church before joining the Shepherds Trail back to Carisbrooke.

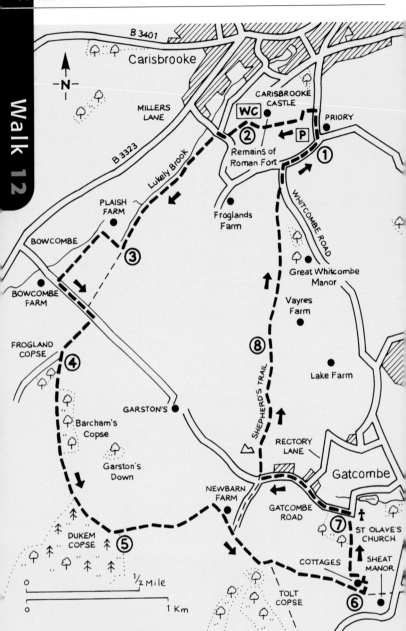

Walk 12 Directions

① From the car park, and facing **Carisbrooke Priory**, turn left and walk along the road. Take the first left-hand footpath and veer left

after a few steps, climbing gently through the trees. On reaching **Carisbrooke Castle**, bear left and follow the path alongside the castle walls. Turn left towards the car park and follow the public footpath sign for **Millers Lane**.

② Turn right on reaching the road, pass Millers Lane and walk to a stile and path on the left, signposted 'Bowcombe'. Cross the field to the next stile and keep going across the pastures, crossing several more stiles. Level with **Plaish Farm** and make for a stile and junction ahead.

③ Bear right here and follow the enclosed path, bending left after a few moments. On reaching **Bowcombe Farm**, turn left and follow the sign for **Gatcombe**. Pass a footpath on the left and continue on the track as it curves right, avoiding the track running straight ahead. Veer away from the track at the corner of **Frogland Copse** and follow the field edge to a gate.

WHERE TO EAT AND DRINK ⓘ
Try the **tea room** at Carisbrooke Castle (open April–October) or at Little Gatcombe Farm in Gatcombe. There are various pubs and cafés in Carisbrooke.

---

the lane, keep right along the bridleway. At the edge of **Tolt Copse** ignore the path right and bear left, soon to leave the Shepherd's Trail, keeping ahead along a bridleway towards **Sheat Manor**.

⑥ Before the manor, at a junction of paths, turn left, following the path past cottages, then bear left again and keep to the curving path as it ascends to woodland. Proceed through the wood and descend to a lane beside **St Olave's Church**.

⑦ Turn left along **Gatcombe Road**, pass **Rectory Lane**, then turn right at a crossing of ways, rejoining the **Shepherd's Trail** for **Carisbrooke**. Pass between properties and climb quite steeply through trees. Pass over a track, go through a gate and follow the path round the left-hand field edge.

⑧ Go through another gate and keep beside the field boundary. The path becomes enclosed by a fence and hedge before reaching a sign for **Carisbrooke** and **Whitcombe Road**. Keep to the obvious path and eventually you reach a junction. Walk ahead to reach the car park.

WHAT TO LOOK FOR ⓘ
Take a closer look at the monks' church, a majestic building with a soaring tower, at **Carisbrooke Priory**. Note the massive Norman pillars and the beautiful angel tomb of Lady Wadham, Jane Seymour's aunt. Peaceful **Gatcombe** has a 13th-century church, containing lovely stained glass, an ancient wooden effigy of a crusader knight, and choir stalls carved from oaks grown in Gatcombe Park.

---

④ Pass through the trees to a gate and continue ahead up the slope, skirting the field boundary. Keep ahead in the next field and head for the gate and bridleway sign. Walk along the edge of **Dukem Copse** and look for a turning on the left to **Gatcombe**.

⑤ Go through a gate and continue along the field edge. On reaching a path to **Garstons**, descend to the right and then swing left to a gate. Follow the bridleway for **Gatcombe** and turn right to **Newbarn Farm**. Bear right at the entrance and, at

---

WHILE YOU'RE THERE ⓘ
Visit **Carisbrooke Castle**. Walk the battlements and savour the majestic view over the surrounding countryside, locate the two medieval wells, one with winding gear driven by a donkey, see the Carisbrooke Castle Story in the gatehouse and discover more about the history of the island in the Isle of Wight Museum in the Great Hall.

Walk 13

Alfred's Ancient Capital

Winchester's historic streets, Cathedral Close and the beautiful Itchen Valley.

•DISTANCE•	3½ miles (5.7km)
•MINIMUM TIME•	1hr 30min
•ASCENT / GRADIENT•	499ft (152m)
•LEVEL OF DIFFICULTY•	
•PATHS•	Established riverside paths through water-meadows, 3 stiles
•LANDSCAPE•	City streets, riverside, water-meadow and downland
•SUGGESTED MAP•	aqua3 OS Explorer 132 Winchester
•START / FINISH•	Grid reference: SU 486294
•DOG FRIENDLINESS•	Under control through water-meadows and by golf course
•PARKING•	Pay-and-display car parks in city centre
•PUBLIC TOILETS•	The Broadway, Winchester

BACKGROUND TO THE WALK

Winchester, ancient capital of Wessex and England, lies steeped in history in the heart of the Hampshire countryside. First settled in the Iron Age and influenced by royalty since the 7th century, the city boasts some remarkable architectural treasures.

Beginning from the imposing bronze statue of King Alfred the Great, who made the city his capital, this delightful walk incorporates some of Winchester's most famous sights, with a stroll through the water-meadows to the Hospital of St Cross and St Catherine's Hill.

Historic Centre

From the Victorian Guildhall, you walk up the High Street, which has been a main thoroughfare to a crossing point on the River Itchen for some 2,500 years, before reaching the Cathedral Close. The magnificent cathedral was founded in 1079 on the site of an earlier Saxon building and remodelled in the 14th century. It is the longest medieval church in Europe and among its treasures are the 12th-century illuminated Winchester Bible, medieval wall paintings and the tombs of early English kings and more recent notables, including Jane Austen and Izaak Walton.

In the close you will find half-timbered Cheyney Court, formerly the Bishop's court house. Beyond Kingsgate you'll pass the entrance to Winchester College, founded in 1382 by William of Wykeham, the oldest school in England. Join one of the guided tours (in summer only) to view the handsome courtyards and cloisters, the chapel with its early 16th-century stained glass window, and to savour the unspoilt medieval atmosphere. At the end of College Street you'll see the Bishops of Winchester's house, the surviving wing of a grand palace built in 1684 overlooking the striking ruins of the 12th-century Wolvesey Palace.

Set in the wide, lush water-meadows beside the Itchen, at the end of the beautiful riverside walk beside the College grounds, is the Hospital of St Cross. Founded in 1132, it still functions as an almshouse and is the oldest charitable institution in the country. Here you can visit the fine Norman church, the Brethrens Hall and medieval kitchen, and take the 'Wayfarer's Dole' – bread and ale – a tradition that survives from the Middle Ages.

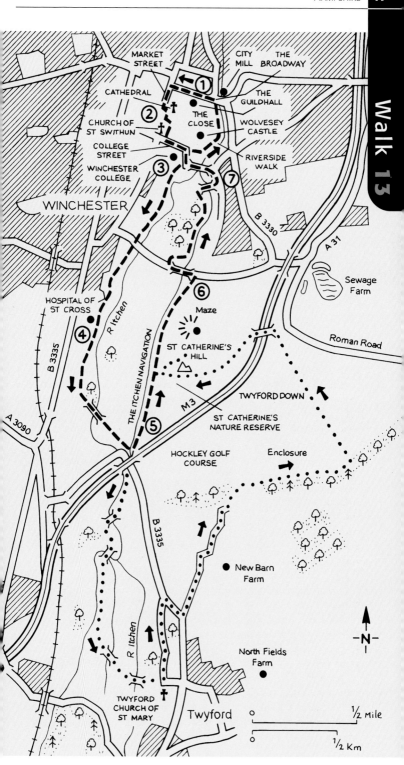

MARKET STREET

CITY MILL

THE BROADWAY

①

CATHEDRAL

THE GUILDHALL

②

THE CLOSE

WOLVESEY CASTLE

CHURCH OF ST SWITHUN

COLLEGE STREET

WINCHESTER COLLEGE

③

RIVERSIDE WALK

⑦

WINCHESTER

B 3330

A 31

Sewage Farm

HOSPITAL OF ST CROSS

R Itchen

⑥

Maze

Roman Road

④

B 3335

ST CATHERINE'S HILL

THE ITCHEN NAVIGATION

M3

TWYFORD DOWN

A 3090

⑤

ST CATHERINE'S NATURE RESERVE

HOCKLEY GOLF COURSE

Enclosure

B 3335

New Barn Farm

-N-

R Itchen

North Fields Farm

TWYFORD CHURCH OF ST MARY

Twyford

½ Mile

½ Km

Walk 13 Directions

① From **King Alfred's statue** on the **Broadway**, walk towards the city centre, passing the **Guildhall** (tourist information centre) on your left. Join the **High Street**, then in 100yds (91m), turn left along **Market Street**. Continue ahead into the **Cathedral Close** to pass the cathedral main door.

WHERE TO EAT AND DRINK ⓘ

Old pubs, tea rooms and restaurants abound around the cathedral and its close. Try the excellent **Cathedral Refectory** or the **Courtyard Café** behind the Guildhall, or the **Wykeham Arms**, in Kingsgate Street, for atmosphere, imaginative food and Hampshire ales.

---

② Turn left down a cloister, then right through the **Close**, (signed to 'Wolvesey Castle'), to **Cheyney Court** and exit via **Prior's Gate**. Turn left though **Kingsgate**, with the tiny **Church of St Swithun** above, then bear left down **College Street** and shortly pass the entrance to **Winchester College**. Beyond the road barrier, bear right along **College Walk**, then turn right at the end of the wall, along a track.

③ Go left through a gate by a private entrance to the **College**. Follow the path beside the **River Itchen** for ½ mile (800m) to a gate

---

WHAT TO LOOK FOR ⓘ

St Catherine's Hill, Winchester's most prominent landmark, is well worth the detour as you head back into the city. It was the site of the area's first settlement and on its summit are the rampart and ditch of an Iron Age hill fort, the Norman remains of St Catherine's Chapel, and a 17th-century turf-cut maze. You'll also be rewarded with excellent views of the city.

---

and road. Cross over and follow the gravel path, alongside a tributary, to a gate and cross open meadow towards the **Hosptial of St Cross**.

④ Keep left alongside the wall and through an avenue of trees to a stile. Proceed ahead along the gravel path to two further stiles and join a farm track leading to a road. Turn left and walk the length of the now gated road (traffic-free), crossing the **River Itchen** to reach a junction of paths by the M3.

⑤ Turn left along a path. Pass a gate on your right (access to **St Catherine's Hill**). Keep left at a fork and drop down to follow a narrow path by the **Itchen Navigation**. Go through the car park to the road.

WHILE YOU'RE THERE ⓘ

Allow time to visit Winchester's **City Museum** on the edge of the Cathedral Close. It tells the story of the city, as an important Roman town and the principal city of King Alfred, through Anglo-Saxon and Norman England to modern times.

---

⑥ Turn left across the bridge and take the footpath immediately right. Keep to the path beside the water, disregarding the path left (College nature reserve). Soon cross the bridge by rowing sheds to join a metalled track,

⑦ Turn left, then left again at the road. Follow the road left along **College Walk** then bear right at the end, signed 'Riverside Walk'. Pass the **Old Bishops Palace** (**Wolvesey Castle**) and follow the metalled path beside the Itchen and up steps to **Bridge Street**, opposite the **City Mill** (now owned by the National Trust). Turn left back to **King Alfred's statue**.

With the Romans and Celts at Farley

A secluded walk through 2,000 years of history on the Greensand ridge.

•DISTANCE•	5 miles (8km)
•MINIMUM TIME•	2hrs 30min
•ASCENT / GRADIENT•	574ft (175m) ▲▲▲
•LEVEL OF DIFFICULTY•	🚶 🚶 🚶
•PATHS•	Forest tracks and rutted lanes, running in water after rain
•LANDSCAPE•	Remote wooded hillsides, occasional farms and cottages
•SUGGESTED MAP•	aqua3 OS Explorer 145 Guildford & Farnham
•START / FINISH•	Grid reference: TQ 051448
•DOG FRIENDLINESS•	Can mainly run free, on lead on roadside section
•PARKING•	Forest car park (number 8) on Farley Heath
•PUBLIC TOILETS•	None on route

BACKGROUND TO THE WALK

High on windswept Farley Heath, you're standing close to the remains of a Romano-Celtic temple, one of the few Roman sites to have been found in Surrey. In Roman times, you'd have got here along the branch road that led north west from Stane Street – the busy London to Chichester highway – at present day Rowhook, on the outskirts of Horsham. You'll cross the line of the road near Winterfold Cottage, and again on Ride Lane, just after the junction with Madgehole Lane.

Pick 'n' Mix Religion

The Romans had a plethora of religious beliefs. They venerated Rome and the Emperor, as well as Jupiter and other Graeco-Roman gods; in far flung outposts like Britain they also embraced the local and pagan religions. By the 3rd and 4th centuries Christianity was gaining ground, and there was increasing interest in mystical religions like the cult of Mithras, the ancient Persian light god.

Both Roman and native gods were worshipped together in Britain, and distinctive Romano-Celtic temples were evolved to accommodate the various different religions. These designs consisted of a square or rectangular tower surrounded by a lean-to verandah, and they were quite unlike other buildings in the Roman landscape.

Uncovering the Past

Farley was typical, and you can see the outline of its foundations just a few paces north of the car park at the start of your walk. The two concentric masonry squares are a modern reconstruction, built to show the ground plan that was discovered by Martin Tupper in 1848, and confirmed by subsequent excavations in 1939 and 1995. The temple itself was built before the end of the 1st century AD. It was enclosed within a precinct wall, or *temenos*, which was also located during the excavations but has since been re-buried. Tupper's finds, which included several decorated bronze strips from a priest's sceptre, are now in the British Museum.

The temple was fairly isolated, although there was a Roman villa just south of Pitch Hill, some 3 miles (5km) back down the road towards Stane Street. No other permanent buildings have been found inside the temple precincts, but the site would have been the focus of regular religious rites, and possibly occasional markets or fairs as well. The temple remained in use until the end of the Roman occupation early in the 5th century, and it seems that the building burnt down some time before the year 450.

Walk 14 Directions

① Stand in the car park facing the road and walk to the entrance on your right-hand side. Cross the road, and follow the signposted public bridleway across **Farley Heath**. Keep to the right at the first fork, and continue straight across when you get to the the sandy bridleway crossroads.

Keep straight on again at the five-way junction, and take the fork to the right a few paces further on. Then, as the main track swings round hard to the left, continue down the waymarked woodland footpath straight ahead. You'll wind gently down to a waymark post; turn right here, and follow the public bridleway for a further 70yds (64m) to a T-junction with **Madgehole Lane.**

Walk 14

② Turn right and follow this deeply rutted, sunken lane until it meets a narrow tarmac road at a pretty, tile hung cottage.

③ Turn left, signposted towards **Winterfold**, and climb through this delightful, sequestered valley past the rambling, half-timbered **Madgehole Farm** to **Madgehole**. Here you leave the tarmac and swing hard right, climbing steadily past a young Christmas tree plantation on your left. Follow the waymarked bridleway as it winds right, then left, through **Great Copse**, and join the **Greensand Way** as it swings in from your right.

WHERE TO EAT AND DRINK ⓘ

You won't find any refreshment stops on this route, so I'd recommend that you pack a drink and a chocolate bar at the very least. After your walk, follow the road towards Shere. Just beyond the railway bridge you'll come to the pink-washed **William IV** at Little London, a 16th-century free house with flagstone floors and a huge inglenook fireplace. They serve good home cooked food (though not on Sunday evenings) together with a decent range of real ales.

④ Turn left onto **Row Lane** and, after 150yds (137m), fork right towards Ewhurst and Shere. Follow the road over the brow of the hill, until you come to car park 5 on your right. Turn left here, onto an unsignposted footpath into the woods, and keep right at the fork 90yds (82m) further on. Almost at once, bear left off the main track, up a narrow footpath by the side of a wire fence. This leads you down beside the huge garden of **Winterfold Cottage**, to another waymarker post. Fork left here, and follow the public bridleway along the rough cottage drive until you reach **Row Lane**.

WHILE YOU'RE THERE ⓘ

After seeing the temple, you might be curious to know what a Roman priest's headdress looked like. Well, you can see one in **Guildford museum**. Right next to the Castle Arch in Quarry Street, you'll find Surrey's largest collection of archaeology and local history; everything from Palaeolithic hand axes to a super collection of 17th-century pottery and glass. The needlework displays include samplers, patchwork and baby clothes, and the museum also features pictures and artefacts illustrating most aspects of local life. The museum is open Monday to Saturday, and admission is free.

⑤ Cross over and continue along the bridleway. After 200yds (183m) it bears hard right onto **Ride Lane**, which will carry you all the way to **Farley Green**. Keep right at the junction with **Madgehole Lane**, and trudge steadily through this rutted, prehistoric landscape until gradually the banks roll back as you approach **Farley Green Hall Farm**.

⑥ Pass the old half-timbered farmhouse on your right, and keep bearing left until you come to the top of the green. Bear left again, and follow **Farley Heath Road** for the final stretch back to your car.

WHAT TO LOOK FOR ⓘ

I saw dozens of **rooks** foraging in the fields as I tramped down Ride Lane towards Farley Green. Rooks return to established breeding sites year after year, building their large, sprawling nests in tall trees such as beech or oak. It's not unusual to find 50 or more nests in a single rookery. There's an old saying that, if you see two crows, then they're actually rooks. The crow always seems to be a much more solitary bird than the noisy, gregarious rook. If you want to be certain of telling these large black birds apart, then look for the rook's conspicuous bare cheeks at the base of the bill.

The Six Wives of Crowhurst

A lovely circular route on the trail of Henry VIII – and another man's wives!

•DISTANCE•	5 miles (8km)
•MINIMUM TIME•	2hrs
•ASCENT / GRADIENT•	131ft (40m) ▲ ▲ ▲
•LEVEL OF DIFFICULTY•	🚶 🚶 🚶
•PATHS•	Farm tracks and well-maintained field paths, some road walking, 10 stiles
•LANDSCAPE•	Gentle, well-farmed landscape
•SUGGESTED MAP•	aqua3 OS Explorer 146 Dorking, Box Hill & Reigate
•START / FINISH•	Grid reference: TQ 365453
•DOG FRIENDLINESS•	Will need to be on lead along roads, through farmyards, and near livestock. Large dogs may have difficulty with stiles
•PARKING•	Adjoining cricket field or in Tandridge Lane, Crowhurst
•PUBLIC TOILETS•	None on route

BACKGROUND TO THE WALK

What a gloriously remote part of Surrey this is! That assertion may strike you as somewhat improbable when you leave your car near the traffic lights, just a stone's throw from the busy A22. But trust me; a few hundred yards (metres) of road walking is a small price to pay for your admission ticket to this little-known corner of the county.

Courting Anne Boleyn

Nowadays, Crowhurst is on the way to nowhere at all, but apparently things were different in the 16th century. According to tradition, Henry VIII would stop over at Crowhurst Place on his way to court Anne Boleyn, who was living just over the Kentish border at Hever Castle. Even then, Crowhurst Place was not new. The lovely timbered and moated manor may be a spectacular example of what most of us loosely call 'Tudor', but it was already half a century old when that dynasty was ushered in on Bosworth Field in 1485.

Enough of the foreplay – you'll want to know about all those wives! The Gaynesford family first pop up during Edward III's reign, when John and Margery Gaynesford received the Manor of Crowhurst from the de Stangrave family. But it was another John Gaynesford – the Sheriff of Surrey, no less – whose dogged pursuit of an heir was to bring him an unbroken run of 15 daughters from his first five wives. His persistence was eventually rewarded when, at long last, he managed to father a son by his sixth wife.

The Gaynesford (later Gainsford) family lasted some 300 years at Crowhurst Place, and it's worth the short diversion to see their tombs, flanking the chancel of Crowhurst's little medieval church. There's also a 15th-century brass likeness of the John Gaynesford who was Surrey's Parliamentary representative in 1431.

Flagging in the Mud

Two hundred years later, one of John's descendants left an altogether different memorial of his own. We know from the 17th-century parish register that, in those days, it was 'a loathsom durtie way every steppe' from Crowhurst Place to the church. Tiring of these muddy pilgrimages, yet another John Gainsford paid £50 to have a stone-flagged causeway laid along the entire route. He got his money's worth, for the causeway still exists in places.

By the dawn of the 20th century Crowhurst Place was bearded with brambles, lonely and unloved. Its saviour was George Crawley, whose comprehensive restoration in 1920 even extended to the brand new mock-Tudor gatehouse on Crowhurst Road. Crowhurst Place isn't open to the public, but you'll see Crawley's handiwork clearly enough from the path, which runs within 100yds (91m) of the house.

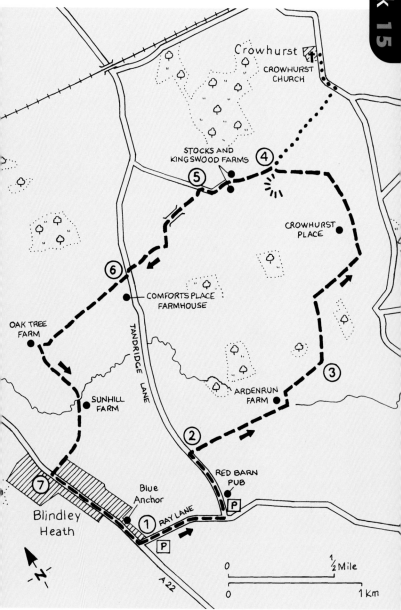

Walk 15 ‍**Directions**

① Turn right out of the car park, and follow **Ray Lane** as far as **Tandridge Lane**. Turn left, pass the **Red Barn** pub, then turn right up the tree lined drive towards **Ardenrun**.

② Walk up the long straight drive until it swings to the left. Follow it for a further 80yds (73m) then, just before the private drive to **Ardenrun Farm**, swing hard right at the yellow waymark onto the '**Age to Age' walk**. Continue for another 300yds (274m).

③ Nip over the stile on the left and walk through two gently rising fields. Turn right at the yellow '**Age to Age**' waymark – where there are good views behind you - and follow the well-maintained path straight across the drive to **Crowhurst Place**. Continue beside the hedge on your right, cross a small footbridge, then head diagonally across the next field to the junction of two farm tracks. There are more good views from this spot and, if you want to visit **Crowhurst church**, you should turn right for 700yds (640m), then left onto **Crowhurst Road**.

④ Turn half left here, and follow the track towards **Stocks and Kingswood Farms**. Leave the 'Age to Age' route, and carry straight along the yellow waymarked track that winds through **Kingswood** farmyard, through a small wooden gate, and along the gravelled drive to the picture-postcard **Stocks Farm house**.

⑤ The gravelled drive joins a surfaced lane at the farm gate; turn left here and, after 20yds (18m), turn left again, over two stiles in quick succession. Head diagonally across the next field, and turn left over the stile. Cross a bridge and a second stile, then keep left until you cross another stile and a small footbridge. Now turn right, walk through two fields, and rejoin **Tandridge Lane**.

⑥ Turn left and, after 55yds (50m), branch off to the right at the entrance to **Comforts Place Farmhouse**. As the drive swings round to the left, nip over the stile and continue along the grassy lane to the rural crossroads at **Oak Tree Farm**. Turn left here, and follow the unmade track past **Highfield House** and out onto a muddy lane. Beyond **Sunhill Farm** the road surface improves, and the lane leads you back to the busy A22.

⑦ Turn left, and follow the main road for the last 800yds (732m) into **Blindley Heath** and back to the car park.

WHERE TO EAT AND DRINK ⓘ

You won't go hungry in Blindley Heath, which boasts two pubs offering extensive all-day menus. Despite its situation next to a filling station on the busy A22, the low, weatherboarded **Blue Anchor** is set well back from the road in its own gardens. With quarry tiled floors and winter log fires, it still retains some of the charm of a genuine country pub. By contrast, the busy family atmosphere of the **Red Barn** in Tandridge Lane rather offsets its quieter situation. But it's horses for courses, and this popular Brewer's Fayre outlet offers a large garden with a nice children's play area.

Wilmington's Mystery of the Long Man

This magnificent downland walk visits a legendary chalk figure which has baffled archaeologists and historians for hundreds of years.

•DISTANCE•	6¼ miles (10km)
•MINIMUM TIME•	2hrs 30min
•ASCENT / GRADIENT•	465ft (152m) ▲▲ ▲
•LEVEL OF DIFFICULTY•	👥 👥 👥
•PATHS•	Downland paths and tracks, stretch of country road, 1 stile
•LANDSCAPE•	Dramatic downland on east side of Cuckmere Valley
•SUGGESTED MAP•	aqua3 OS Explorer 123 South Downs Way – Newhaven to Eastbourne
•START / FINISH•	Grid reference: TQ 543041
•DOG FRIENDLINESS•	Some of enclosed tracks suitable for dogs off lead
•PARKING•	Long stay car park at Wilmington
•PUBLIC TOILETS•	At car park

BACKGROUND TO THE WALK

One of Britain's most impressive and enduring mysteries is the focal point of this glorious walk high on the Downs. Cut into the turf below Windover Hill, the chalk figure of the Long Man of Wilmington is the largest representation of the human figure in western Europe and yet it remains an enigma, its origins shrouded in mystery. For centuries experts have been trying to solve this ancient puzzle but no one has been able to prove conclusively who he is or what he symbolises.

Helmeted War-god

For many years the earliest record of the Long Man was thought to have been a drawing by the antiquarian William Burrell, made when he visited Wilmington Priory in 1766. Then, in 1993, a new drawing was discovered, made by John Rowley, a surveyor, as long ago as 1710.

Though the new drawing has confirmed some theories, it has not been able to shed any real light as to the Long Man's true identity or why this particular hillside was chosen. However, it does suggest that the original figure was a shadow or indentation in the grass rather than a bold line. It seems there were distinguishing facial features which may have long faded; the staves being held were not a rake and a scythe as once described and the head was originally a helmet shape, indicating that the Long Man may originally have been a helmeted war-god.

Until the 19th century the figure was only visible in a certain light, particularly when there was a dusting of snow or frost on the ground. The Long Man's ghostly aura, the chill, wintry conditions and the remoteness of these surroundings would surely have been enough to send a shiver down the spine. In 1874, a public subscription was raised through the Times and the figure re-cut. To help define the outline of the Long Man, the site was marked out in yellow bricks, though this restoration work may have resulted in the feet being incorrectly positoned.

Camouflaged

In 1925 the Long Man of Wilmington was given to the Sussex Archaeological Trust, which later became the Sussex Archaeological Society, and during World War II the site was camouflaged to prevent enemy aircraft from using it as a landmark. In 1969 further restoration work began and the yellow bricks were replaced with pre-cast concrete blocks. These are frequently painted now, so that the shape of the Long Man stands out from a considerable distance away.

Photographed from the air, the figure is elongated, but when viewed from ground level an optical illusion is created and he assumes normal human proportions. The walk passes as close as it can to the Long Man before heading out into isolated downland country where the trees of Friston Forest can be seen cloaking the landscape.

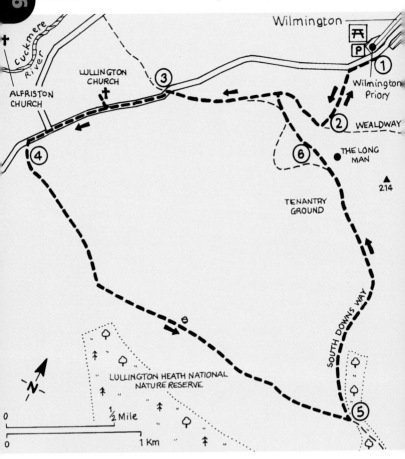

Walk 16 **Directions**

① Make for the car park exit and follow the path parallel to the road, heading towards the **Long Man**. Bear left at the next gate and take the **Wealdway** to the chalk figure. Climb quite steeply, curving to the right. Go through a gate, avoid the **Wealdway** arrow and go straight ahead towards the escarpment, veering right just below the **Long Man**.

Walk 16

② Go through the next gate, cross a track and bear left on reaching a fence. A few paces brings you to a gate and a sign for the **South Downs Way**. Pass a small reservoir and follow the track to the road.

③ Turn left and walk down to a signpost for **Lullington church**, following the path alongside several cottages. After visiting the church, retrace your steps to the road and turn right. Head down the lane and look for **Alfriston church** on the right. Pass a turning to the village on the right and continue ahead towards **Seaford**. Look out for a post box and swing left here, signposted '**Jevington**'.

> **WHERE TO EAT AND DRINK** ⓘ
> At the far end of the car park, where the walk starts and finishes, is a very pleasant picnic area. The **Giant's Rest** in Wilmington is a popular pub at the northern end of the village. They serve soup, ploughmans lunches, jacket potatoes or rabbit and bacon pie.

④ Follow the bridleway as it climbs steadily between tracts of remote downland. Keep left at the next main junction and there is a moderate climb. Avoid the bridle track branching off to the left and continue ahead towards Jevington. **Lullington Heath National Nature Reserve** is on the right now. Pass a bridleway to **Charleston Bottom**

> **WHILE YOU'RE THERE** ⓘ
> Make a detour to look at the **Lullington Heath National Nature Reserve**, which consists of scrubland, chalk grassland and the best example of chalk heath still surviving in Britain. Various heathers and orchids also grow here. Study the maps displayed along the reserve boundary to help you follow the reserve's paths and bridleways.

on the right and keep on the track as it climbs quite steeply. Pass a second sign and map for the nature reserve and make for a junction with the **South Downs Way**.

⑤ Turn left and follow the enclosed path to a gate. Go straight ahead alongside woodland and pass through a second gate. The path begins a gradual curve to the left and eventually passes along the rim of a spectacular dry valley known as **Tenantry Ground**. Keep the fence on your left and look for a gate ahead. Swing right as you approach it to a stile and then follow the path alongside the fence, crossing the top of the **Long Man**.

⑥ Glance to your right and you can just make out the head and body of the chalk figure down below. It's an intriguing view. Continue keeping the fence on the right and descend to a gate. Turn right here and retrace your steps to the car park at **Wilmington**.

> **WHAT TO LOOK FOR** ⓘ
> **Wilmington Priory**, by the car park, was founded for the Benedictine abbey of Grestain in Normandy, and much of the present building dates from the 14th century. As few as two or three monks resided here and they used the parish church in Wilmington rather than build their own place of worship. The monks were engaged in managing the abbey's English estates. The priory is in the care of the Landmark Trust and used as a holiday let. It is not open to the public. Only 16ft (5m) square, 13th-century **Lullington church** stands on a hill above the Cuckmere valley and is one of the smallest churches in the country. It was originally a much larger church and it's not clear why much of it was destroyed but only part of the chancel remains.

Romans and Normans at Pevensey

Visit a Norman castle within a Roman fort and experience the atmosphere of the eerie Pevensey Levels on this fascinating walk.

•DISTANCE•	4½ miles (7.2km)
•MINIMUM TIME•	1hr 45min
•ASCENT / GRADIENT•	Negligible
•LEVEL OF DIFFICULTY•	
•PATHS•	Field paths, brief stretch of road and riverside, 4 stiles
•LANDSCAPE•	Low level former marshland, flat and watery landscape
•SUGGESTED MAP•	aqua3 OS Explorer 124 Hastings & Bexhill
•START / FINISH•	Grid reference: TQ 645048
•DOG FRIENDLINESS•	Under control on farmland and minor roads
•PARKING•	Pay-and-display car park by Pevensey Castle
•PUBLIC TOILETS•	At car park

BACKGROUND TO THE WALK

The great harbour here silted up long ago, leaving Pevensey stranded inland, 2 miles (3.2km) from the sea. It was from here that William, Duke of Normandy marched inland to defeat King Harold and his Saxon army in 1066. What took place represents one of the most significant events in English history.

Roman Fortress

The exact spot where William came ashore can never be identified, as the coastline has shifted and altered so greatly down the centuries. What is known, however, is that 800 years before the arrival of William, the Romans chose this site to construct the fortress of Anderida as part of their defence of the Saxon Shore. Pevensey was one of a series of fortifications along this coast and the remains of the outer walls of the castle survive. Standing up to 30ft (9m) thick in places and enclosing an oval area of about 10 acre (4ha), the walls are considered to be among the finest examples of Roman building in the world.

In 1066, centuries after the Roman invasion of Britain, William, Duke of Normandy crossed the Channel and came ashore at Pevensey. Determined to claim the English crown, he expected to be met with some resistance at Anderida. But William found the fort undefended, enabling him to consolidate his position immediately. Harold and his men were elsewhere, fighting his brother's Danish army in Yorkshire and expecting William to sail via the Isle of Wight.

The Normans immediately set about erecting one of three prefabricated timber castles they had brought with them, constructing it on a mound of earth within the fort. It was as if they were intent on taking the place of the Romans who had occupied this site so many years before them. Without opposition, the Norman army travelled almost casually through the Sussex countryside, taking food from local people and burning and looting whatever they could find. Following the Battle of Hastings, William gave the stronghold to his half brother, Robert, Count of Mortain. It was Robert who built the Norman castle, the remains of which we see today. A keep and bailey were subsequently constructed and in the 13th century a formidable stone curtain wall and gatehouse were added.

Further Defences

Further work took place in the 14th century but by now the castle was sturdy enough to defend itself and its inhabitants from the strongest opponent. Pevensey was prepared to defend the coast from the threat of Napoleon and even as recently as 1940, pill boxes were installed into the castle walls should German forces invade.

    This wonderfully atmospheric walk starts at Pevensey Castle, which the tourist blurb aptly describes as 'a battle-scarred witness to 17 centuries of turbulent history.' After a brief tour of Pevensey, with its picturesque houses and cottages, head out across the lonely, evocative Pevensey Levels, once covered by water and now reminiscent of the fenland country of East Anglia.

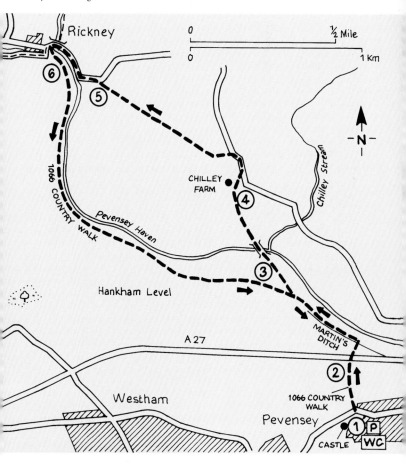

Walk 17 **Directions**

① On leaving the car park, go straight ahead on the bend and keep the **Priory Court Hotel** on the right. The castle walls rise up on your left. Bear off to the right just beyond the hotel to follow the **1066 Country Walk**.

② Cross the A27 and keep on the trail, following the sign for **Rickney**. Go through two gates and follow the path as it bends left. Continue between fencing and hedging; keep **Martin's Ditch** on the left and pass through a galvanised gate. Make for a signpost and veer off diagonally right, leaving the **1066 Country Walk** at this point.

③ On reaching the riverbank footpath sign, at the confluence of the **Pevensey Haven** and the **Chilley Stream**, continue for a short distance to a footbridge. Cross it and aim half left, making for a house. Head for a gap in the line of bushes and then cross rough, thistle-strewn ground to two stiles in the corner by some trees. Bear right to a galvanised gate, then turn left and cross the field, keeping a house on your left. On reaching a gate, turn right and walk along the track to the road.

> ### WHERE TO EAT AND DRINK ⓘ
> **Priory Court Hotel** near the car park has a selection of hot and cold food, as well as a restaurant and beer garden. Cumberland sausage, lasagne, steak and kidney pudding and chilli con carne are among the dishes. The **Royal Oak** and the **Smugglers** also serve food and the **Castle Cottage Restaurant** and tea room is very popular.

④ Swing left at the lane and follow it until it curves right. Go through a gate on the left here, reaching a second gate just beyond. Follow the path to some gates and pass through the right-hand one. Keep ahead to a gate in the field corner and continue, keeping the boundary on your left. Make for a footbridge on the left. Cross it and bear right. Follow the edge of the pasture to two stiles and exit to the road.

> ### WHILE YOU'RE THERE ⓘ
> Take a stroll through ancient Pevensey and visit the **Court House Museum** in the High Street, once the smallest town hall in England. In 1882, under the Municipal Corporation Act, Pevensey lost its status as a borough and in 1890 the Pevensey Town Trust was established to administer the Court House. Inside, you can see the Court Room, Robing Room, cells and exercise yard. There are many exhibits and displays, including a silver penny of William I, minted at Pevensey.

⑤ Keep left and walk along to the village of **Rickney**. Avoid the 1066 Country Walk as it runs off to the north and cross the little road bridge. Bear left at the sign for **Hankham** and immediately cross a bridge. Swing left after a few paces and follow the **1066 Country Walk**.

⑥ Go through a galvanised gate and follow the path as it heads for the **Pevensey Haven**. Make for another gate and continue beside or near the water. On reaching a gate, keep ahead and look for a finger post, indicating a path on the right. Avoid the path and continue ahead, still on the **1066 Country Walk**. Retrace your steps to the A27, cross over and return to **Pevensey**.

> ### WHAT TO LOOK FOR ⓘ
> By the **Pevensey Castle** car park entrance is a plaque to commemorate a visit by Her Majesty Queen Elizabeth II on 28 October 1966 and the landing of William, Duke of Normandy on 28 September 1066. A former coastal inlet which was drained mainly in the 14th and 15th centuries, the **Pevensey Levels** have their own individual character. This is a haven for wildlife, plants and insects, as well as home to a great variety of birds, both in summer and winter. Redshank, plovers, snipe and wildfowl visit in winter, while skylarks and kestrels are found here throughout the year.

Great Dixter and its Glorious Gardens

A very pleasant walk on the Sussex/Kent border, highlighting the skill and creativity of a famous architect and a gifted gardening writer.

•DISTANCE•	3½ miles (5.7km)
•MINIMUM TIME•	1hr 30min
•ASCENT / GRADIENT•	98ft (30m) ▲ ▲ ▲
•LEVEL OF DIFFICULTY•	🏃 🏃 🏃
•PATHS•	Field paths and quiet roads, 11 stiles
•LANDSCAPE•	Undulating farmland and stretches of woodland
•SUGGESTED MAP•	aqua3 OS Explorer 125 Romney Marsh, Rye & Winchelsea
•START / FINISH•	Grid reference: TQ 828245
•DOG FRIENDLINESS•	Dog stiles near Great Dixter and on Sussex Border Path
•PARKING•	Free car park on corner of Fullers Lane and A28, Northiam
•PUBLIC TOILETS•	Great Dixter. Seasonal opening

BACKGROUND TO THE WALK

Deep in the tranquil, rolling countryside of East Sussex, close to the Kent border, lies Great Dixter, one of the county's smaller and more intimate historic houses.

Family Theme
Built in the middle of the 15th century and later restored and enlarged by Sir Edwin Lutyens, Great Dixter is a popular tourist attraction as well as a family home. These days this fine Wealden hall-house is owned and cared for by Olivia Eller and her uncle Christopher Lloyd, the gardening writer. It was Christopher's father, Nathaniel, who instructed Lutyens in 1910 to make major changes to Great Dixter, which at that time was in a poor state of repair. His main task was to clear the house of later alterations and, typically, the work was undertaken with great sensitivity.

But Lutyens didn't stop there. While all the restoration plans were beginning to take shape he and Nathaniel Lloyd seized on another opportunity to improve and enlarge the house. A complete timber-framed yeoman's hall at Benenden in Kent, scheduled for demolition, was skilfully dismantled piece by piece and moved to Great Dixter, adding an entire wing to the house.

One of Great Dixter's most striking features is the magnificent Great Hall, the largest surviving timber-framed hall in the country. Visitors never fail to be impressed by its medieval splendour. The half timbered and plastered front and the Tudor porch also catch the eye. The contents of Great Dixter date mainly from the 17th and 18th centuries and were collected over the years by Nathaniel Lloyd. The house also contains many examples of delicately fashioned needlework, which were completed by his wife Daisy and their children.

Impressive Gardens
However, a tour of Great Dixter doesn't end with the house. The gardens are equally impressive. Christopher Lloyd has spent many years working on this project, incorporating

many medieval buildings, establishing natural ponds and designing yew topiary. The result is one of the most exciting, colourful and constantly changing gardens of modern times. As with the house, plans were drawn up to improve the gardens, and here Lutyens was just as inventive. He often used tiles in a decorative though practical manner, to great effect. At Great Dixter he took a chicken house with crumbling walls and transformed it into an open sided loggia, supported by laminated tile pillars.

Beginning in Northiam, the walk heads round the edge of the village before reaching the house at Great Dixter. Even out of season, when the place is closed, you gain a vivid impression of the house and its Sussex Weald setting. Passing directly in front of Great Dixter, the route then crosses rolling countryside to join the Sussex Border Path, following it all the way back to Northiam.

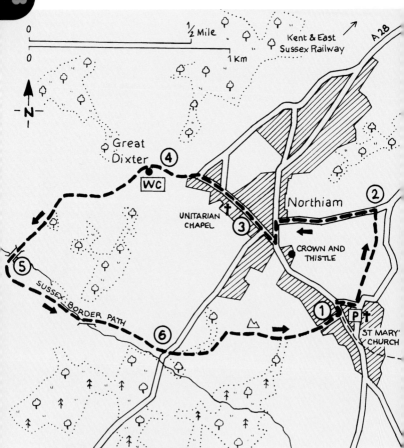

Walk 18 **Directions**

① Turn right out of the car park and walk along **Fullers Lane** towards **St Mary's Church**. Take the path on the left, signposted to

Goddens Gill, and keep to the right edge of the field. Cross a stile in the corner and look for an oasthouse on the right. Make for a path on the far side of the field and follow it between fences towards a thatched cottage. Cross a stile to the road.

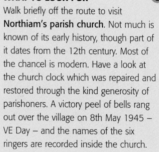

Walk 18

② Turn left and head for the A28. Bear left and walk along to the **Crown and Thistle**. From here cross the road and take the turning signposted 'Great Dixter'. Pass a telephone box and go straight on at the crossroads, following **Great Dixter Road**.

③ Pass the **Unitarian Chapel** and avoid the path on the right. Keep left at the junction with **Higham Lane** and continue to follow the signs for **Great Dixter**. Disregard a turning on the right and go straight on, following a path between trees and hedges, parallel to the main drive to the house.

④ Pass the toilets and head towards a cattle grid. Cross the stile just to the left of it and follow the path signposted to **Ewhurst**. Follow the waymarks and keep the hedge on the left. Cross a stile in the field corner and then head diagonally down the field slope to the next stile. Follow the clear path down the field slope.

⑤ Make for a footbridge and then turn left to join the **Sussex Border Path**. The path skirts the field before disappearing into woodland. Emerging from the trees, cut straight across the next field to two stiles and a footbridge. Keep the woodland on the left and look for a gap in the trees. Cross a stream to a stile and bear right. Follow the right edge of the field and keep on the **Sussex Border Path** until you reach the road.

⑥ Cross over the lane to a drive. Bear immediately left and follow the path to a stile. Pass alongside woodland and then veer slightly away from the trees to a stile in the approaching boundary. Cross it and go straight ahead up the field slope. Take the first footpath on the right and follow it to a gap in the field corner. Cross a footbridge under the trees and continue along the right-hand edge of the next field to join a drive. Bear left and follow it to the road. Turn left, then right to return to the car park at **Great Dixter**.

Walk 19

Corridors of Power

A look at some of the city's landmarks, from Whitehall through to Smithfield.

•DISTANCE•	4 miles (6.4km)
•MINIMUM TIME•	2hrs 30min
•ASCENT / GRADIENT•	Negligible ▲ ▲ ▲
•LEVEL OF DIFFICULTY•	🚶 🚶 🚶
•PATHS•	Paved streets
•LANDSCAPE•	Main processional routes, busy streets
•SUGGESTED MAP•	AA Street by Street London
•START•	Westminster tube
•FINISH•	Farringdon tube
•DOG FRIENDLINESS•	A dog's nightmare
•PUBLIC TOILETS•	Westminster, Strand

BACKGROUND TO THE WALK

It's easy to take sights for granted in a city where, around every bend, is another symbol of its historic importance. Hopefully, this walk, through some of the better-known parts, will sharpen your senses and alert you to some of the buildings and streets you may be familiar with, and others that you have yet to notice. It's best to avoid this walk on Mondays when some of the places mentioned are closed.

The walk begins across the road from the Houses of Parliament at Westminster Abbey, where every king and queen since 1066 has been crowned and where many are buried. On a corner opposite Horse Guards Parade is one of the best places to stand for a grandstand view of the Queen's carriage as it heads up Whitehall for the State Opening of Parliament. We move on to the Strand, once one of the most influential thoroughfares in Britain with many fine mansions, some of which you can still see today. One of these is the magnificent Somerset House, which has awesome grounds for central London and is much-loved by film companies for its grandeur and seclusion.

The street names from here on give a clue to the past inhabitants. Think of dukes and earls – Arundel, Surrey and Essex – as the Strand enters Aldwych (a name that derives from 'Old Wic' meaning old settlement). The grand buildings in this area are symbols of the architectural legacy of the Empire. If you're after proof, notice how Canada House, the South African Embassy and the Australian High Commission each take pride of place in Trafalgar Square, the Strand and Aldwych respectively. Where the Strand ends and Fleet Street begins are a number of banks. These serviced those working at the Inns of Court, including Lloyds Bank with its floral tiles, and Child & Co Bankers. The latter has a display of guns in a cabinet that the partners of the bank acquired during the Gordon Riots of 1780 'for the defence of the building'. Here too is one of the first cheques – made out in 1705.

We end the walk by another church, St Bartholomew-the-Great, which dates from 1123 and is still surrounded by small streets as it was in the Middle Ages. Near by is Smithfield, the scene of jousting, tournaments and fairs and the site for executions where criminals were not just hanged but boiled, roasted or burnt. During the Peasant's Revolt of 1381 the rebel leader Wat Tyler was stabbed by the Lord Mayor William Walworth and taken to St Bartholomew's Hospital but soldiers dragged him out and decapitated him.

Walk 19 Directions

① Leave **Westminster tube** following signs to the Houses of Parliament. Cross **Abingdon Street** to **Westminster Abbey** and the adjacent St Margaret's Church. Turn back along Abingdon Street and continue ahead as the road becomes **Parliament Street**, and then **Whitehall**. Follow it past the Cenotaph, a simple block of Portland Stone that commemorates those people who died in the First and Second World Wars, all the way to **Trafalgar Square**.

② Turn right here and cross **Northumberland Avenue**. Turn right into the **Strand**, the road that links Westminster with the City of London. Turn right at **Savoy Street**, to see the Queen's Chapel of the Savoy; otherwise carry on along the Strand, past **Somerset House**.

Walk 19

③ Turn right into **Surrey Street**, past the Roman Baths, left into **Temple Place** and left again along **Arundel Street**. The two churches in the middle of the road are St Mary-le-Strand and St Clement Danes. After these the road becomes **Fleet Street**.

④ After the banks of Lloyds and Child & Co turn right into **Whitefriars Street**. At the end turn left and left again into **Dorset Rise**. Take the next right into Dorset Buildings, past the Bridewell Theatre and along **Bride Lane** to St Bride's Church. Cross **New Bridge Street**.

⑤ You are now in Ludgate Hill. Turn left into the street called **Old Bailey** and continue to the Central Criminal Court, known as 'The Old Bailey' – it lies on the site of the notorious former Newgate Prison.

Cross **Newgate Street** and follow **Giltspur Street** to reach St Bartholomew's Hospital.

⑥ Walk under the archway to the hospital, with the only remaining sculpture of Henry VIII, to visit St Bartholomew-the-Less, the parish church of the hospital where the Stuart architect Inigo Jones was baptised. As you continue past the central square opposite Smithfield Market, notice the marks on the stone wall left by a Zeppelin raid during the First World War. At St Bartholomew-the-Great turn left into **Hayne Street** and again into **Charterhouse Street**.

⑦ At **St John Street** turn right and then bear left into **St John's Lane**. A few paces further on you will find **St John's Gate**. Keep going to reach Grand Priory Church, bear left to **Jerusalem Passage**, then turn left at the end, on to **Aylesbury Street**. Cross **Clerkenwell Street** and walk along **Britton Street**, turning right into **Benjamin Street** to reach **Farringdon tube** where the walk ends.

The Flaming City

A linear walk tracing the route of the Great Fire of 1666, an event that created a demand for new furniture.

•DISTANCE•	2¼ miles (3.6km)
•MINIMUM TIME•	2hrs
•ASCENT / GRADIENT•	Negligible
•LEVEL OF DIFFICULTY•	
•PATHS•	Paved streets
•LANDSCAPE•	Alleys and roads in busy City of London
•SUGGESTED MAP•	AA Street by Street London
•START•	Monument tube
•FINISH•	Farringdon tube
•DOG FRIENDLINESS•	Not a good one for dogs
•PUBLIC TOILETS•	Monument, Mansion House

BACKGROUND TO THE WALK

Londoners in the 17th century must have wondered what had hit them when, within months of fighting off the Great Plague, a fire of monumental proportions began at a bakery in Pudding Lane. It was 2AM in the morning on 2 September 1666 when the baker discovered the fire. He escaped to safety along a roof, but his young assistant was not so lucky. Neither were the 13,000 houses, 87 churches and 40 livery halls that perished in the flames but, incredibly, only eight people lost their lives, although how many later died after being left homeless is unknown. It took five days to contain the fire, partly because of the high number of houses with timber roofs and the rudimentary fire-fighting equipment available at the time.

Cabinet Decision

The event at least offered an opportunity to give the City a facelift but, due to the sheer cost and to property rights, most of the rebuilding followed the original street lines. It did, however, create a safer, more sanitary capital than before, and with the new houses came a demand for new furniture, which was excellent news for cabinet-makers.

Rebuilding the Home

Within six years the City had been rebuilt, its boundaries extended and London was in the midst of an economic boom. By 1700 the population had increased five-fold to 500,000 inhabitants and, in terms of technical development, the city's manufacture of chests and cabinets led the way. Perhaps one of the most common items produced by a cabinet-maker was the table, candlestands and mirror ensemble, which had been introduced from France and soon became a standard item of furniture in many English homes. Cabinets were made by skilled craftsmen and therefore more expensive. However, the same techniques were later used for chests of drawers. To meet heavy demands furniture was, for the first time, offered across a range of quality and price.

Brisk trade with North America, the East Indies, East India and the Far East introduced new styles such as lacquer-ware. Although France led the way in furniture design, Oriental items such as screens were very popular. Most Londoners made do with 'japanned' furniture that was varnished in a cheaper imitation of lacquer, many of which survive today. Cane chairs too, were introduced from the Far East and most middle class homes had one or more of these so-called 'English chairs'. With the demand for furniture of all types and to match all pockets, the working life of a tradesman in the late 1600s was a happy one indeed.

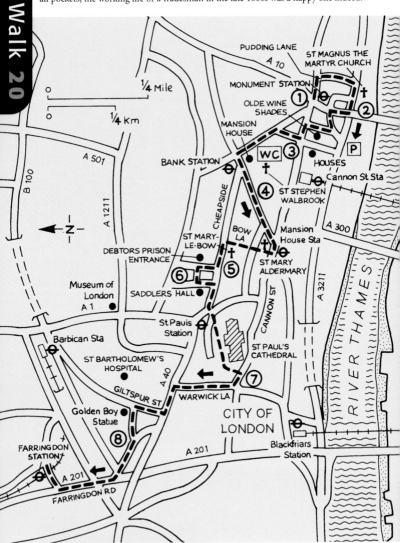

Walk 20 **Directions**

① Take the **Fish Street Hill** exit from the tube station and bear right towards the **Monument**. Then follow the cobbled street for 20yds

(18m) to see the plaque that marks the spot on the corner of **Pudding Lane** where the ill-fated bakery once stood. Bear right, then cross **Lower Thames Street** at the pedestrian crossing to reach **St Magnus the Martyr Church**.

Walk 20

② A few paces further to the right of the church, climb a set of steps and, ignoring the first exit, continue to arrive on the west side of **London Bridge**. Continue ahead, away from the river, along **King William Street** and shortly turn left along **Arthur Street** and then sharp right into **Martin Lane**, past the Olde Wine Shades. At the end turn left into **Cannon Street**. (For a detour to see the red brick houses that survived the fire, turn next left into Laurence Poultney Hill.)

> **WHILE YOU'RE THERE**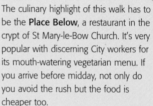
> Head for the **Museum of London** in nearby London Wall to find out more about the Great Fire and the devastation witnessed by Samuel Pepys. This is the world's largest urban history museum – it offers an insight into London life from the Roman era to the 18th century. Many artefacts are on display, including a tiny crucifix delicately carved from bone by an inmate of Newgate Prison.

③ Cross the road and turn right into **Abchurch Lane**. At the end bear left along **King William Street** towards Bank tube station. Keep to the left, past the front of Mansion House, and notice the street on the left, Walbrook: this is the site of one of Wren's finest churches, St Stephen Walbrook Church. Turn left into **Queen Victoria Street**.

④ Continue ahead, then turn right into **Bow Lane**, past St Mary Aldermary and a row of shops, to St Mary-le-Bow at the end. Turn left into **Cheapside** which, despite being the widest road in the City, also went up in flames.

⑤ Cross this road, turn right into **Wood Street** and take the narrow alley on the right, **Milk Street**. Follow it round to enter a courtyard

> **WHERE TO EAT AND DRINK**
> The culinary highlight of this walk has to be the **Place Below**, a restaurant in the crypt of St Mary-le-Bow Church. It's very popular with discerning City workers for its mouth-watering vegetarian menu. If you arrive before midday, not only do you avoid the rush but the food is cheaper too.

with an eerie entrance to the old debtors' prison. Carry on through the alley, to the left of the **Hole in the Wall** pub, to rejoin Wood Street.

⑥ Cross the road into **Goldsmith Street** and, at the Saddlers Hall opposite, turn left and rejoin **Cheapside**. Turn right and cross the pedestrian crossing to St Paul's Cathedral. Walk through the churchyard, bear left to reach **Ludgate Hill** and turn left.

⑦ Turn right and right again into **Ava Maria Lane**, which becomes **Warwick Lane**. At the end turn left along **Newgate Street**. At the traffic lights turn right along **Giltspur Street**, then left into **Cock Lane**.

⑧ Where another road meets it, turn right along **Snow Hill Lane**, past an angular building, and continue along **Farringdon Road**. At the traffic lights turn right, to reach **Farringdon tube**, where the walk ends.

> **WHAT TO LOOK FOR**
> The statue on the building at the corner of Cock Lane of the 'Golden Boy' marks the spot where the fire is thought to have ended. On this site, until 1910, stood a pub called The Fortune of War where body-snatchers would leave bodies on benches and wait to hear from the surgeons of the nearby St Bartholomew's Hospital.

Walk 21

Harwich's Seafarers and Wanderers

An easy town walk discovering Harwich's exciting maritime past.

•DISTANCE•	4 miles (6.4km)
•MINIMUM TIME•	1hr 30min
•ASCENT / GRADIENT•	Negligible
•LEVEL OF DIFFICULTY•	
•PATHS•	Town streets and promenade with gentle cliffs
•LANDSCAPE•	Coast, beach, cliffs and town
•SUGGESTED MAP•	aqua3 OS Explorer 197 Ipswich, Felixstowe & Harwich
•START / FINISH•	Grid reference: TM 259328
•DOG FRIENDLINESS•	Between 1 May and 30 September dogs have to be on lead on promenade and cliff walks
•PARKING•	Free car parks at Ha'penny Pier and informal street parking
•PUBLIC TOILETS•	Beside Quayside House opposite Ha'penny Pier

BACKGROUND TO THE WALK

One of the main gateways to the Continent, Harwich is a must for aficionados of all things maritime. The town lies beside the grey North Sea on an isthmus between Dovercourt and Bathside bays, overlooking the Stour and Orwell estuaries and drew not only invaders and traders to its shores but adventurers and explorers too. In the 12th century a violent storm caused the rivers to break their banks and form the promontory where Harwich stands today. Realising its strategic importance the lord of the manor developed the site into a walled town. You can see the remains of his wall in St Nicholas' churchyard.

The walk begins at the Ha'penny Pier where you can spot ferries sailing to and from Europe, against a backdrop of giraffe-like cranes rising from the flat Felixstowe coast. Keeping the sea to your left you'll see traditional inns, such as the Globe, in Kings Quay Street. Such pubs were once stormed by press gangs who kidnapped boys for service in the Royal Navy. Trying to escape forceable enlistment, hapless lads would scurry like rats into the labyrinthine passages linking the houses, but many were caught and never seen again.

Famous Visitors

The town has played host to some famous faces too. Sir Francis Drake dropped in on his way to Spain and Queen Elizabeth I stayed here, remarking that 'It is a pretty town that wants for nothing'. Diarist Samuel Pepys was the local MP and Lord Nelson sojourned here with Lady Hamilton. Home-grown boys include Christopher Jones, captain of the *Mayflower*, the ship in which the Pilgrim Fathers sailed from Plymouth to the Americas in 1620.

Wander at will and see the quirky, two-wheel man operated treadwheel crane on Harwich Green or climb the Redoubt, built to fend off a threatened Napoleonic invasion, for great sea views. Along the seafront is a pair of 19th-century lighthouses. The first is the Low Lighthouse, now the Maritime Museum and the other, just 150yds (137m) inland, is the High Lighthouse. They were built by General Rebow, a get-rich-quick entrepreneur who charged each ship a penny per ton to come into port. When Rebow got wind that the sandbanks were shifting he craftily sold the lighthouses to Trinity House. On the way to Dovercourt you'll pass Beacon Hill Fort, dating back to Roman times, although the gun emplacements here are of World War One and World War Two vintage. As you round the breakwater there are fine beaches and another pair of cast iron lighthouses mounted on stilts, built to replace the earlier ones at Harwich. They, too, became redundant (in 1917) but serve as yet another reminder of Harwich's seafaring history.

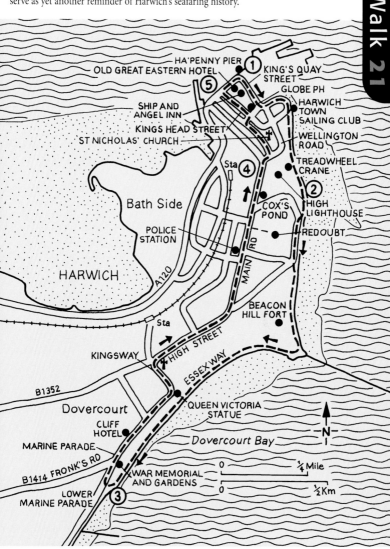

Walk 21 **Directions**

① With your back to **Ha'penny Pier** turn left along **The Quay** and follow the road into **Kings Quay**

Street. Turn left just before the colourful mural, painted by the Harwich Society and Harwich School in 1982 and again in 1995, which depicts local buildings and ships. Follow the road, with the sea on your left, until it turns inland. Take the path by the sea, which is the start of the **Essex Way**, a long distance path of 81 miles (130km) connecting Harwich with Epping. Pass **Harwich Town Sailing Club** and maintain direction along the **Esplanade** where at low tide you can walk along the shingle beach.

② Pass the **Treadwheel Crane** on your right and continue along the seafront taking care along the sloping concrete walkway. Keep the raised, fenced area of **Beacon Hill Fort** and the gun emplacements from World War One and World War Two to your right. As you pass the breakwaters around the bay there are views of the holiday resort of Dovercourt. Ignore the steps to your right and continue along the **Essex Way**, walking parallel with the upper road of **Marine Parade** on your right.

> **WHAT TO LOOK FOR** ℹ
> Look for two quite different walls. One is the **Flint Wall** in Kings Head Street, made from ship's ballast, and the other is the remains of the 12th-century **town wall**. The latter is in St Nicholas' Churchyard, opposite the vestry door, where at ground level you can see part of a wall built of septaria, a poor quality stone dredged out of the local estuaries.

③ Turn right into **Lower Marine Parade** and pass the **War Memorial and Gardens** at the junction with Fronk's Road and Marine Parade. Maintain direction passing the **Cliff Hotel** on the left and then go left into **Kingsway**, opposite the statue of Queen Victoria. Turn right into the **High Street** and bear left into **Main Road**, passing the police station on your left. Walk for 250yds (229m) and turn right up the track to see the **Redoubt**, a

> **WHILE YOU'RE THERE** ℹ
> Visit **St Nicholas' Church** built of pale yellow brick in simple Gothic style. Crusaders prayed here before leaving for their journey to the Holy Land; royalty worshipped here on their way to the Continent; and other luminaries, such as Willoughby, Drake, Nelson, Samuel Pepys and Daniel Defoe almost certainly dropped in when they lodged at Harwich.

Martello-style fort, part of the defences against Napoleonic invasion. Continue to pass **Cox's Pond**, once owned by local bankers of the same name. They are better known in military circles as Cox and Kings, the Army bankers.

④ Pass **High Lighthouse** on the right, turn right into **Wellington Road** and left into **Church Street** passing St Nicholas' Church. Turn right into **Market Street** and left into **Kings Head Street**, pausing to admire the timber-framed Elizabethan houses including No 21, the home of Christopher Jones, captain of the *Mayflower*.

⑤ Turn right into **The Quay**, where Quayside Court faces the sea. Now a block of apartments, Quayside Court was built as one of the Great Eastern hotels in the 19th century and catered for travellers from the Continent who would arrive by steamer at what is now Trinity Quay and continue their journey to London by rail.

> **WHERE TO EAT AND DRINK** ℹ
> There are plenty of pubs to choose from, many dating back to the 16th and 17th centuries. Options include the **Globe** in Kings Quay Street one of the oldest buildings in Harwich, the **Angel Inn** and the **Ship Restaurant** next to the shipyard and the Alma Inn, a former wealthy merchant's house.

Plague Strikes in Ashwell

See evidence of the bubonic plague before strolling along the chalky downs.

•DISTANCE•	6½ miles (10.4km)
•MINIMUM TIME•	2hrs 30min
•ASCENT / GRADIENT•	140ft (43m) ▲ ▲ ▲
•LEVEL OF DIFFICULTY•	🚶 🚶 🚶
•PATHS•	Tracks and paths, some lanes around Ashwell, 1 stile
•LANDSCAPE•	Arable chalk downs and muddy plain
•SUGGESTED MAP•	aqua3 OS Explorers 193 Luton & Stevenage; 208 Bedford & St Neots
•START / FINISH•	Grid reference: TL 268396 (on Explorer 193)
•DOG FRIENDLINESS•	Mostly arable land, some cattle approaching Ashwell
•PARKING•	East end of High Street, outside United Reformed church
•PUBLIC TOILETS•	Recreation Ground off Lucas Lane

BACKGROUND TO THE WALK

One of the most moving things you will see on any of these walks is the graffiti on the north wall inside the tower of St Mary's Church in Ashwell. High up the wall is a graffito inscription in Latin which translated says 'The first plague was in 1349', and lower down a more desperate one, 'Miserable, wild, distracted, the dregs of the people alone survive to witness, 1350' while the last in the series refers to a great storm, 'At the end of the second (plague) a tempest full mighty this year 1361 St Maur thunders in the heavens'.

Black Death

The graffiti bear a remarkable witness to the Black Death, the bubonic plague spread by black-rat fleas, that swept into England from the Continent and Asia in 1348. It was devastating, particularly as the harvests had failed repeatedly since 1314 and already large areas were unploughed. It is thought that a third of the population died in the first outbreaks. No-one was immune: the Abbot of St Albans, Michael of Mentmore, and 47 of his monks died of the plague in April 1349 alone. The scrawlings give an awesome insight into the state of mind of Ashwell's residents, but the January storms, which did great damage and would have seemed to be the final blow, probably cleared out the plague for a while and gave the community a chance to recover.

Defiant Spike

The church tower, under construction at the time of the plague, is in chalk stone and thus easily incised and carved. There are other equally interesting pieces of graffiti, including a 15th-century drawing of old St Paul's Cathedral in London and, elsewhere in the church, one by a bitter mason or builder which translates 'The corners are not pointed (mortared) correctly – I spit'.

The tower is an immense piece of work – one could speculate that it eventually rose as a defiance or commemoration of the tribulations of the village. At 176ft (54m), it is seen for miles around with its three storeys, massive angle buttresses and crowning 'Hertfordshire spike' spire. Ashwell itself is an exceptionally interesting village. There is a museum in an early 16th-century, timber-framed building, originally built as the local estate office for the Abbey of Westminster, which owned the manor until 1540. Ashwell was a market town and one of five in the county recorded in the Domesday Book. Ashwell's open fields remained unenclosed until as late as 1863. To the west, Caldecote is a deserted, medieval village whose economic viability probably received a serious setback from the Black Death. Owned by St Albans Abbey, it was deserted by 1428 and now consists of just a moated manor house (rebuilt around 1500) and a small church.

Walk 22 **Directions**

① Walk west down **Ashwell High Street**, eventually curving left to ascend to a junction. Turn right into **Hinxworth Road**. Shortly after passing the gates to **West Point**, go straight on to a track at a bridleway sign, the road bearing right.

② The track climbs **Newnham Hill** with fine views back to Ashwell church tower and long views northwards. Descend to a bridleway junction. Turn right alongside the hedge, then turn left at a footpath post to go through the hedge and continue westward.

WHERE TO EAT AND DRINK ℹ️

Ashwell's several pubs include the **Rose and Crown** (also a restaurant) and the **Three Tuns Hotel** in the High Street; also here is the **Thirty One Tea Rooms**. You could try the **Bushel and Strike** in Mill Street. On the route there is the **Three Horseshoes** at Hinxworth.

---

③ Beyond some former farm cottages turn right on to a concrete road to walk past **Caldecote Manor** and **St Mary's Church** (not open to the public). Follow the road until just before **Meadow Cottages**. Here go left to skirt a copse, then go straight on along a track between fields. When you reach a deep ditch, go left a few paces to cross it. Carry on going straight ahead, aiming for the left end of a hedge, turning right to walk alongside it, and then through pasture.

④ At the lane go straight on past the medieval **Hinxworth Place** to skirt to the right of some scrub. Now go diagonally across some

---

WHAT TO LOOK FOR ℹ️

The Black Death that ravaged Ashwell may have fatally weakened nearby **Caldecote**, a small manor of 325 acres (132ha) owned by St Albans Abbey and deserted after 1428. The manor house, church and a cottage incorporating the old rectory are all that remain today. Many villages with 'cold' in their name were deserted in the late Middle Ages. Often they are located in bleak, exposed locations or on poor land.

---

arable land, heading for **Hinxworth Church**. Go through a hedge to walk alongside a deep ditch and then left over a footbridge. Go along a field edge before turning right into the churchyard via a kissing gate.

⑤ Leave the churchyard along a short lime avenue, turning left to walk up **High Street**, past the quirky war memorial clock tower. Turn right into **Chapel Street**. At a footpath sign go right on to a cinder track which curves left to pass between two cottages, then through vast arable fields. At a crossroads go past some farm buildings to descend across more arable land. Having crossed a footbridge over the **River Rhee**, go diagonally left in a pasture to cross another bridge. Now turn left along the field edge.

WHILE YOU'RE THERE ℹ️

About 6 miles (9.7km) away from Ashwell, over the border in Bedfordshire, you could round off the day with a trip to the **Shuttleworth Collection** at Old Warden, west of Biggleswade. Started in 1928, it is a superb collection of vintage aircraft and road vehicles, all in airworthy or roadworthy condition.

---

⑥ At a lane go left past a cottage and opposite go right, with a moat in the field on your left. Turn right on to a lane and, where this turns right, go left, the path curving right through farmland to a stile. Once over this stile turn right and continue along a lane, carrying straight on into **Rollys Lane**.

⑦ At the T-junction go right into **Mill Street** and visit the church. Cross **Swan Street** to the path beside **Ashwell Village Museum**, and back to **High Street**.

Blenheim Palace Parkland

A fine walk in peaceful countryside to one of Britain's top country houses.

•DISTANCE•	7 miles (11.3km)
•MINIMUM TIME•	3hrs
•ASCENT / GRADIENT•	150ft (46m) ▲ ▲ ▲
•LEVEL OF DIFFICULTY•	👫 👫 👫
•PATHS•	Field paths and tracks, parkland paths and estate drives. Some quiet road walking, 3 stiles
•LANDSCAPE•	Farmland and parkland
•SUGGESTED MAP•	aqua3 OS Explorer 180 Oxford
•START / FINISH•	Grid reference: SP 411158
•DOG FRIENDLINESS•	On lead in grounds of Blenheim Palace
•PARKING•	Spaces in centre of Combe
•PUBLIC TOILETS•	Blenheim Palace, for visitors; otherwise none on route

BACKGROUND TO THE WALK

When King George III first set eyes on Blenheim Palace, he remarked, 'We have nothing to equal this.' Few would disagree with him. The views of the palace, the lake and the Grand Bridge from the waterside path on this delightful walk are stunning. Set in a magnificent 2,000-acre (810ha) park landscaped by 'Capability' Brown, the great Baroque house covers a staggering 7 acres (2.8ha) and is England's largest stately home.

Blenheim Palace took nearly 20 years to build and was finally completed in 1722. The architect John Vanbrugh was commissioned to design the house for John Churchill, 1st Duke of Marlborough (1650–1722), following his victory over the French at Blenheim in 1704. Inside, there are various state rooms and tapestries, the Long Library – considered by many to be the finest room in the house – and the room where Winston Churchill was born in 1874.

A Just Reward

It was Queen Anne who decided that John Churchill's efforts in battle should be suitably rewarded, reflecting the high regard in which the nation held him. But what exactly did Churchill do to earn such respect? As a soldier and as a statesman, he was responsible for supressing Louis XIV's grand imperialist ambitions in Europe. His spirit and determination resulted in a crushing and humiliating defeat of the French at Blenheim on 13 August 1704. Though he had achieved his objective, Churchill was not ready to retire from the battlefield and he went on to secure many more victories in his illustrious career.

In gratitude, Queen Anne conferred the Royal Manor of Woodstock on the Duke of Marlborough and his heirs in perpetuity, and a sum of £500,000 was voted by parliament for the building of Blenheim Palace. But problems lay ahead. The Duke's wife, Sarah, was Princess Anne's favourite companion before she became Queen in 1702. Sarah used her close friendship and her influence in royal circles to secure a dukedom for her husband, and it was she, not the Duke of Marlborough, who approved the plans and then supervised the building work. Proving just how ruthless and determined she could be, Sarah rejected Sir Christopher Wren's designs in favour of those produced by John Vanbrugh.

A Sweet House

The Duchess remained a thorn in the side of builders and architects for some time, insisting that all she wanted was a 'clean, sweet house and garden, be it ever so small.' Parliament complained about the spiralling cost, money gradually ran out and the Duchess forbade Vanbrugh from seeing the finished building in 1725, refusing him entry to the grounds.

Characterised by ornament and exuberance, creating a memorable skyline, Blenheim Palace – decidedly not 'ever so small' – is not to everyone's taste, though the immense scale of the house has to be seen as a tribute to the skill and ingenuity of its creators. The vast parkland and gardens, too, are renowned for their beauty and range. Vanbrugh's Grand Bridge is the focal point, but elsewhere there are formal water terraces and an arboretum – among many other features.

Walk 23 **Directions**

① From the green, take the road signposted 'East End'. Swing right by the village pump into the churchyard and keep to the left of the church. Exit through the gap in the boundary wall, flanked by two gravestones, and begin skirting the right-hand edge of the sports field. After about 50yds (46m), branch off into the trees, then head diagonally across the field. Cross into the next

Walk 23

field and keep to the right edge of the wood. In the next field, turn left, still with trees on the left, and go up the slope to the woodland corner. Pass through a gap in the hedge and cross the field.

② Exit to the road, turn left and keep right at the next junction. Walk along to **Combe Gate**. Go through the large kissing gate into the grounds of **Blenheim Palace**, keep left at the junction and follow the drive through the parkland. As it sweeps left to a cattle grid, veer off to the right by a sign 'visitors are welcome to walk in the park'. Follow the grassy path to a stile. Keep right when the path divides and walk beside the western arm of **The Lake**.

③ Eventually you reach a tarmac drive. Turn right and walk down towards the **Grand Bridge**. As you approach it, turn sharp left, passing between mature trees with **Queen Pool** on your right. Cross a cattle grid and keep ahead through the

park. With the **Column of Victory** on your left, follow the drive as it sweeps to the right.

④ Turn left at a cattle grid, in line with the buildings of **Furze Platt** on the right. Join the Oxfordshire Way, cross a stile and follow the grassy track alongside trees, then between fields. At length cross a track and continue towards woodland. Enter the trees and turn left after a few paces to join a clear track running through the wood.

⑤ After about 150yds (137m) take the first left turning, crossing a footbridge to reach the edge of a field. Keep right here, following the obvious path across the fields. When you reach a track, turn right. Keep alongside trees to a junction. Turn right and follow the track down through a wood and diagonally left across a strip of pasture to an opening in the trees. Go up to a track and cross it to a ladder stile.

⑥ Turn left to a hedge, then turn right, keeping it and a ditch on your right. Skirt a field to the road, turn right and walk back into **Combe**.

WHAT TO LOOK FOR
The **Column of Victory** dates back to 1731 and was built to commemorate the heroic efforts of the 1st Duke of Marlborough on the battlefield. Until the mid-19th century, this famous landmark was home to one of the last pairs of breeding ravens in the county.

WHILE YOU'RE THERE
Have a look at **Combe church**. The original building, which was in the valley about 1 mile (1.6km) from its present site, was built during the Norman period. The present church was built or rebuilt in about 1395, about 50 years after the villagers moved their homes up the hill out of the valley. The design of the church is a prime example of the Early Perpendicular style, with a stone pulpit and medieval stained glass. Unusually, the war memorial at Combe gives the dates the men of the village who lost their lives. All except one died in the First World War.

Alfred's Greatness Remembered at Wantage

Visit the statue of a revered British king before heading for spectacular downland country.

•DISTANCE•	6 miles (9.7km)
•MINIMUM TIME•	2hrs 45min
•ASCENT / GRADIENT•	150ft (46m)
•LEVEL OF DIFFICULTY•	
•PATHS•	Pavements, tow path, field paths and tracks, 1 stile
•LANDSCAPE•	Town outskirts, farmland and downland
•SUGGESTED MAP•	aqua3 OS Explorer 170 Abingdon, Wantage
•START / FINISH•	Grid reference: SU 397881
•DOG FRIENDLINESS•	On lead on town outskirts, in villages and if horses about
•PARKING•	Long-stay car park off Mill Street
•PUBLIC TOILETS•	By Town Council offices off Church Street and Portway

BACKGROUND TO THE WALK

King Alfred (AD 849–99) is one of those heroic figures we may remember from the pages of school history books. His victories in battle and his reputation for scholarship and justice rightly earned him the title Alfred the Great. He is suitably commemorated in the Market Place of Wantage, the town of his birth. The striking marble statue of him at its centre was sculpted by Count Gleichen, Prince of Hohenlohne-Langenburg, and unveiled in 1877. As you pass by it, in the initial stages of the walk, note the battleaxe in one hand and manuscript in the other.

Alfred Makes his Mark

Alfred, the youngest son of King Aethelwulf, succeeded his brother Aethelred as Kingin ad 871, at a time when Viking invaders had overwhelmed most of England to the north of the Thames and Wessex was under constant attack. Seven years later Alfred defeated the Danish army at Edington in Wiltshire. He repelled another invasion in 885 and captured London the following year.

Alfred is also remembered for building a fleet, which earned him a reputation as 'father of the English navy,' and creating a ring of fortified strongholds around his kingdom. He was an educated man and as a child he travelled to Rome and to the Frankish court of Charles I, the Bald. He played a key role in reviving and translating many documents and was instrumental in codifying the laws of his kingdom. For example, he made a treaty which recognised the partition of England, with the Danelaw under Viking rule.

A Mighty Battle

But it is the Battle of Ashdown, not far from Wantage, fought in AD 871, with which most local people probably associate Alfred. While the Danes held Reading, it was Alfred's intention to try and entice them away from the river, which they commanded, and confront them on the downs.

Alfred and his brother Aethelred successfully encouraged the enemy to pursue them up the Kennet Valley. The two men then fell back towards the downs with the Danes in hot pursuit. Then, at Ashdown, they stood their ground. What happened next is not clear. The area surrounding the Ridgeway here was guarded by forts and perhaps Alfred looked to them for help in his quest for victory.

Alfred Wins the Day

Whatever took place high on the downs above Wantage, Alfred won the day, sending the Danes packing with the hollow sound of defeat ringing in their ears. Above all, Alfred had taught them a lesson, proving that once they were away from their boats they were an easy target. Alfred scored a number of victories over the Danes before being forced to retreat to the relative safety of the Somerset Marshes. However, he had taken a positive first step in his efforts to resist the Vikings during the following years.

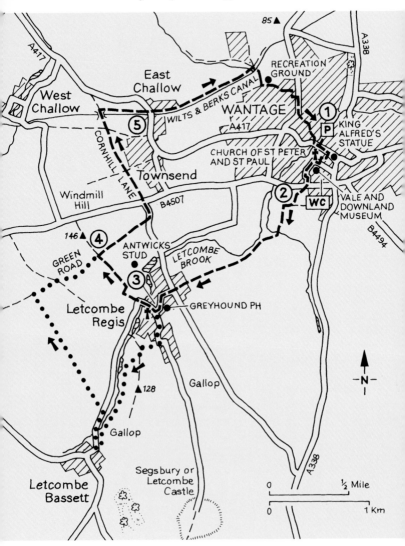

Walk 24 Directions

① Keep to the right edge of the car park and look for the pedestrian exit. Turn left into **Mill Street** and walk up into the **Market Place**. Make for the statue of King Alfred and then follow the signs for the museum. Approach the parish Church of St Peter and St Paul and turn left into **Church Street**. The museum is opposite you at the next junction. Turn right here, avoid Locks Lane and follow **Priory Road** to the left. Head for **Portway** and cross over to a footpath to the left of **The Croft**.

② Follow the clear tarmac path as it runs between fences and playing fields. At length you reach a housing estate; continue ahead into **Letcombe Regis** and make for the junction with Courthill Road. Keep it on your left and go straight ahead through the village, passing the **Greyhound** pub and a thatched cottage dated 1698.

③ Turn right by the church, signposted 'Letcombe Bassett and Lambourn' and, when the road bends sharp left, go straight ahead. After a few paces the drive bends right. Keep ahead along a path between banks of vegetation, following it as it curves right, then swings left. Pass **Antwicks Stud** over to the right and climb gently between trees and bushes.

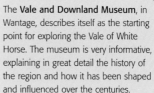

④ Turn right at the next intersection and follow the tree-lined track to the road. Turn left and make for the junction. Cross over, pass alongside a house and follow **Cornhill Lane**. Begin a gentle descent, cross a track and continue down the slope. Avoid the right turning and keep ahead to a footbridge crossing the old Wilts and Berks Canal. Turn right and follow the tow path.

⑤ Cross the **A417** road and continue towards Wantage. Follow a drive and then take the parallel path on the right, running alongside a section of restored canal. On reaching a tarmac drive, turn right and walk along to a row of houses. Turn left at the path junction, pass a recreation ground and follow the path as it curves right. Turn left into **Wasborough Avenue**, then, after some lock-up garages, left into **St Mary's Way**. Turn right and swing left into **Belmont**. Keep right at the fork and make for **Mill Street**. Keep left and the car park is on the left.

Walk 25

Thomas Cromwell and the Destruction of Hailes Abbey

How an important abbey was destroyed by a King's Commissioner.

•DISTANCE•	5 miles (8km)
•MINIMUM TIME•	2hrs
•ASCENT / GRADIENT•	605ft (185m) ▲ ▲ ▲
•LEVEL OF DIFFICULTY•	🚶 🚶 🚶
•PATHS•	Fields, tracks, farmyard and lanes, 7 stiles
•LANDSCAPE•	Wide views, rolling wolds and villages
•SUGGESTED MAP•	aqua3 OS Explorer OL45 The Cotswolds
•START / FINISH•	Grid reference: SP 050301
•DOG FRIENDLINESS•	Mostly on leads – a lot of livestock in fields
•PARKING•	Beside Hailes church
•PUBLIC TOILETS•	None on route

BACKGROUND TO THE WALK

In the decade from 1536 to 1547 just about every English religious institution that was not a parish church was either closed or destroyed – this was the Dissolution, Henry VIII's draconian policy to force the old Church to give up its wealth. The smaller monasteries went first, then the larger ones and finally the colleges and chantries. All their lands and tithes became Crown property. Much of them were sold off to laypeople, usually local landowners. The Church as a parish institution was considerably strengthened as a result of the Dissolution, but at the expense of the wider religious life. The suppression of the chantries and guilds, for example, meant many people were deprived of a local place of worship.

Hailes Abbey

Hailes Abbey was one of the most powerful Cistercian monasteries in the country, owning 13,000 acres (5,265ha) and 8,000 sheep. It was a particular target for reformers. In 1270 Edmund, Earl of Cornwall, the son of its founder, had given the monastery a phial supposed to contain the blood of Christ. Thomas Cromwell was the King's Commissioner responsible for seeing to the closure of the monasteries. He is reputed to have surveyed the destruction of the monastery from a vantage point near Beckbury Camp. There is still a fine view of the abbey from here, as you should find as you pass Point ⑤ on this walk. According to Hugh Latimer of Worcester, who had been working with him, Cromwell also spent an afternoon in 1539 examining the so-called 'blood'. Cromwell concluded that it was nothing more than an 'unctuous gum and compound of many things'. Once the valuables had been removed, local people took what was left. The monastery lands were disposed of in a typical manner. First they were confiscated by the Crown and then sold to a speculator who sold the land on in lots. In about 1600 the site of the abbey was bought by Sir John Tracy, the builder of Stanway House. The monks were dispersed: a few secured positions as parish clergy, whilst others took cathedral posts at Bristol and Gloucester. Others returned to the laity.

Walk 25

Charming Remains

Hailes church is all that remains of the village of Hailes. It predates the abbey and survived the Dissolution, perhaps because it had been a parish church and was not directly linked to the neighbouring monastery. It is a church of real charm, sadly ignored by the many visitors to the monastery's ruins. Although very small, it has several special features, including a panelled chancel – floored with tiles from the monastery – and a nave with 14th-century wall paintings. Didbrook church also survived the upheavals. Built in Perpendicular style, it was rebuilt in 1475 by the Abbot of Hailes, following damage caused by Lancastrian soldiers after the Battle of Tewkesbury.

Walk 25 Directions

① From **Hailes church** turn right and follow the lane to a T-junction. Turn right and after 200yds (183m) turn right on to a footpath. Cross an area of concrete and follow a track as it goes right and left, becoming a grassy path beside a field. Go through a gate, followed by a stile. After about 75yds (69m) turn left, through a gate, and cross a field to a gate at a road.

② Turn right and follow the road as it meanders through the pretty village of **Didbrook** then a stretch

Walk 25

WHAT TO LOOK FOR ℹ️
As you walk through the village of Didbrook, see if the blacksmith at the **Acorn Smithy** is open. In Wood Stanway, the wall of one of the first houses you pass to your left is covered in **vines**, producing a very healthy-looking crop of red grapes in the autumn, even though the English climate tends to favour white grapes.

of countryside. At a junction turn right for **Wood Stanway**. Walk through this village into the yard of **Glebe Farm**.

③ At a gate and a stile cross into a field and walk ahead, looking for a stile on the left. You are now on the **Cotswold Way**, well marked by arrows with a white dot or acorn. Cross into a field and go half right, keeping to the left of some telegraph poles, to a gap in a hedge. Bear half left across the next field, heading towards a house. Cross a stile and turn sharp right, up the slope, to a stile on your right. Cross this and turn immediately left up the field. Go left over a ladder stile by a gate. Follow the footpath as it wends its way gently up the slope. At the top go straight ahead to a gate at a road.

WHERE TO EAT AND DRINK ℹ️
Just near the end of the route is **Hayles Fruit Farm**. You can pick your own fruit, buy a variety of produce from the shop or you can have a light meal in the tea room. Winchcombe is the nearest town, offering many possibilities.

④ Turn right and right again through a gate to a track. Follow this, passing through a gate, until at the top (just before some trees), you turn right to follow another track for 50yds (46m). Turn left through a gate into a field and turn sharp

right to follow the perimeter of the field as it goes left and passes through a gate beside the ramparts of an Iron-Age fort, **Beckbury Camp**. Continue ahead to pass through another gate which leads to a stone monument with a niche. According to local lore, this is the point from where Thomas Cromwell watched the destruction of Hailes Abbey in 1539.

WHILE YOU'RE THERE ℹ️
Visit **Hailes Abbey**. You can rent a recorded commentary that explains the layout of the ruins. **Farmcote church** is another gem, little more than a chapel but ancient and uplifting. It's hard to find but worth the effort. Overlooking Hailes, it's located high up in a silent, tranquil corner of the wolds.

⑤ Turn right to follow a steep path down through the trees. At the bottom go straight across down the field to a gate. Pass through, continue down to another gate and, in the field beyond, head down to a stile beside a signpost.

⑥ Cross this and turn right down a lane, all the way to a road. To the left is **Hayles Fruit Farm** with its café. Continue ahead along the road to return to **Hailes Abbey** and the starting point by the church.

Along Offa's Dyke

Exploring the Saxon King's earthwork along the Celtic border.

•DISTANCE•	4½ miles (7.2km)
•MINIMUM TIME•	2hrs 15min
•ASCENT / GRADIENT•	740ft (225m) ▲▲▲
•LEVEL OF DIFFICULTY•	👣👣 👣👣
•PATHS•	Tracks, fields, lanes, stony paths and riverbank, 5 stiles
•LANDSCAPE•	River, meadows, woodland, farmland and village
•SUGGESTED MAP•	aqua3 OS Outdoor Leisure 14 Wye Valley & Forest of Dean
•START / FINISH•	Grid reference: ST 540011
•DOG FRIENDLINESS•	Off lead for long stretches, but occasional livestock
•PARKING•	Lay-by near telephone box in Brockweir or Tintern Old Railway Station, on other side of river (fee)
•PUBLIC TOILETS•	None on route (except at Tintern Old Railway Station)

BACKGROUND TO THE WALK

Offa's Dyke is a massive earthwork constructed by King Offa, the ruler of the Saxon kingdom of Mercia, in the 8th century AD. The dyke represented the western frontier of his kingdom and ran for about 170 miles (274km) from Chepstow in the south (near the confluence of the Wye and the Severn) to Prestatyn in the north. Its basic construction consisted of a bank of earth, 20ft (6.1m) high and 8ft (2.4m) wide, with a ditch at the foot of its western flank. Even today the frontier between Wales and England runs largely along the course of the dyke. (On this stretch the River Wye forms the present-day boundary between Gloucestershire and Monmouthshire.) The construction of the dyke was felt to be necessary because, after the Romans decamped and the Angles and Saxons invaded, Britain was divided into a number of warring kingdoms. Among these Mercia finally became pre-eminent in England, but the Celtic Britons clung tenaciously to their western mountains. Under Offa, Mercia gradually absorbed other Saxon kingdoms and its King became *de facto* ruler of the English in England.

Definitive Boundary

It is not thought that the dyke was conceived as a fortification – it was more a means of definitively marking the boundary between Mercia and its neighbouring kingdoms. Nor was it the first of its kind. Other Saxon rulers had defined their kingdoms in a similar fashion, but none had done so on the scale undertaken by Offa. There is some variation in build quality throughout its length, but it is nonetheless an impressive achievement for its time. The Offa's Dyke Path, opened in 1971, is more or less the same length as the dyke itself but only rarely do the two coincide precisely.

Brockweir was once the most important port of the River Wye. Together with the River Severn, the River Wye was the main trade route serving the Forest of Dean. Timber, iron and coal from the Forest were brought to Brockweir, loaded at the wharf and shipped downstream to Chepstow. A horse-drawn tram that brought the goods from the mines also served the port. Brockweir was also a centre of shipbuilding. All of this came to an end with the arrival of the railway in the late 19th century.

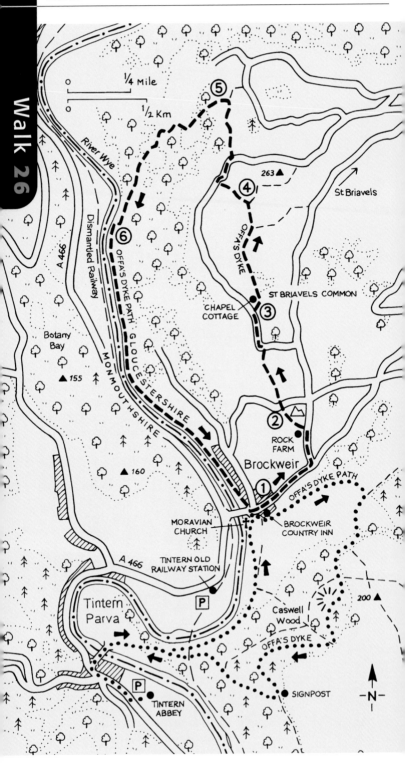

Walk 26 **Directions**

① Walk uphill out of Brockweir until you reach a junction on your left, signposted '**Coldharbour**'. Turn left along this narrow lane for about 160yds (146m). At a corner beside **Rock Farm** turn left on to a track, marked '**Offa's Dyke Path**', which soon narrows markedly and climbs fairly steeply. Keep going up to a lane.

WHERE TO EAT AND DRINK ⓘ

In Brockweir itself is the pretty **Brockweir Country Inn**. Over the bridge and a short distance downstream is **Tintern Old Railway Station**, where a café is open throughout the summer months.

---

② Cross this and continue your ascent until you reach another lane. Turn left here and follow the lane for 200yds (183m), to pass a cottage on the right, followed by some ruined stone buildings. Turn right along a lane.

③ Keep to the right of **Chapel Cottage** on to a path, still ascending. When you reach a wider track, fork left. This dwindles to a path, continuing to climb, until it brings you to another track, beside a stone stile. Turn left again.

④ After a few paces, before a gate and a house, fork right to a stile at a field. Cross this to another pair of stiles, to the left of a house. In the

---

WHAT TO LOOK FOR ⓘ

Near the bridge in **Brockweir** you will probably notice that the water swirls and ruffles for no obvious reason Look more closely and you will see that beneath the water are the remains of the old wharf that was used by trading vessels until the late 19th century.

---

next field stay to the left of a farm and come to a stile at a lane. Turn right and follow this gently climbing lane. It levels out and then, where it starts to climb again at a corner, turn left on to the right-hand path, heading towards Oak Cottage, Bigs Weir and Monmouth. Descend until you arrive at a lane before a house.

⑤ Turn left here to follow a track that descends to the right of another house. This track will continue down into woodland. Stay on the main, obvious track, watching out for loose stones, as it meanders down the hillside. This will bring you to a cottage at a corner. Go left with the track, which later becomes a narrow path. Stay on this and follow it down the side of the hill among trees, still keeping an eye on loose pebbles. Soon the River Wye will appear below you, to the right. At the bottom pass through a gap in the fence, and bear right towards the grassy riverbank, where you will meet a stile.

WHILE YOU'RE THERE ⓘ

In the village of St Briavels is **St Briavel's Castle**. This was built in 1131 by the Earl of Hereford as a centre of administration for the Forest of Dean and the Wye Valley. The castle is not a typical Norman construction as it was never intended as a front-line defensive structure. King John enlarged it in the 13th century and it is now a youth hostel.

---

⑥ Turn left through the stile and follow the river all the way back to Brockweir, passing through gates and crossing bridges where they arise. As you approach the village keep close to the river to enter a path that will bring you on to a lane leading up to the road at **Brockweir Bridge**.

A Pilgrimage Around St Non's Bay

Easy walking around the wonderful coastline that gave birth to the patron saint of Wales.

•DISTANCE•	3½ miles (5.7km)
•MINIMUM TIME•	1hr 30min
•ASCENT / GRADIENT•	262ft (80m) ▲ ▲▲ ▲▲
•LEVEL OF DIFFICULTY•	🚶🚶 🚶🚶 🚶🚶
•PATHS•	Coast path and clear footpaths over farmland, 6 stiles
•LANDSCAPE•	Leafy countryside and dramatic cliffs
•SUGGESTED MAP•	aqua3 OS Explorer OL35 North Pembrokeshire
•START / FINISH•	Grid reference: SM 757252
•DOG FRIENDLINESS•	On lead around St Non's Chapel and well
•PARKING•	Pay-and-display car park in St David's
•PUBLIC TOILETS•	Next to tourist information centre

BACKGROUND TO THE WALK

This walk makes a great evening stroll. The paths that lead from the city are pleasant and easy to follow but as always they're quickly forgotten as you step out into the more glamorous surroundings of the coast. The all-too-short section of towering buttresses and jagged islets leads easily to a spot that can claim to be the very heart of spiritual Wales – the birthplace of St David. The serenity of the location soothes the mind in readiness for the short jaunt back to the compact little city he founded.

Patron Saint

Considering the immense influence he has had on Welsh culture, little is known about the patron saint himself. His mother is said to be St Non, derived from Nun or Nonita, who was married to a local chieftain called Sant. They settled somewhere near Trwyn Cynddeiriog, the rocky bluff that forms the western walls of the bay named after her.

Calming Influence

Legend suggests that David was born around AD 500, in the place where the ruined chapel stands today. Although a fierce storm raged throughout his birth, a calm light was said to have lit the scene. By the morning, a fresh spring had erupted near by, becoming the Holy Well of St Non and visited on this walk. St David went on to be baptised by St Elvis at Porthclais, in water from another miraculous spring.

Man With a Mission

Judging from his parentage, David would have been well educated and it is believed that he undertook a number of religious odysseys, including one to Jerusalem, before he finally returned to his birthplace around AD 550. He then founded a church and monastery at Glyn Rhosyn, on the banks of the River Alun, on the site of the present cathedral, where he set about trying to spread the Christian word to the, mainly pagan, Celts before his death in 589.

St David's Day is celebrated on 1 March every year and St Non, who saw out her life in Brittany, is remembered on the day after.

St David's City

St David's is little more than a pretty village, though it boasts the title 'city' due to its magnificent cathedral. It's a wonderful place and doesn't seem any the worse for the amount of tourism that it attracts. Known as Tyddewi – David's House – in Welsh, the city grew as a result of its coastal position at the western extreme of the British mainland. It would have been linked easily by sea with Ireland and Cornwall. As well as the cathedral and the ruins of the Bishop's Palace, it houses a plethora of gift shops and the National Park information centre, close to the car park, is one of the finest in the country.

Walk 27 **Directions**

① Turn left out of the car park in St David's and walk down the road, as if you were heading for **Caerfai Bay**. As the houses thin out, you'll

see a turning on the right that leads to more dwellings. Take this and then turn left on to a waymarked bridleway. Follow this bridleway between hedges, past the end of a road and on to a junction with another road.

Walk 27

② Walk straight across and take the waymarked path down a pleasant track to a stile. Cross and keep to the left of the field to another stile, where you keep straight ahead again. This leads to a farmyard, which is also a caravan park.

WHERE TO EAT AND DRINK ℹ
Apart from the possibility of an ice-cream van in the car park at Porth Clais, the best bet for refreshment is St David's where there's plenty of choice.
A favourite pub is the **Farmers Arms** on Goat Street, which has a good garden and serves up all the usual pub fare. For non-alcoholic refreshment, try the excellent **Low Pressure Café**.

③ Turn right and keep the hedge on your right, where the drive swings off to the left. Continue across this field and at the end drop down between gorse bushes to the road at **Porth Clais**. Turn left to the bottom of the valley and then, before crossing the bridge, turn left on to the coast path.

④ Climb up steeply on to the cliff tops and bear around to the left to walk towards **Porth y Ffynnon**. The next small headland is **Trwyn Cynddeiriog**, where there's a lovely grassy platform above the cliffs if you fancy a rest. Continue walking into **St Non's Bay** and look for a footpath on the left that leads to the ruined chapel.

⑤ From the chapel, head up to a gate that leads to **St Non's Well** and, from there, follow the path beneath the new chapel and back out on to the coast path. Turn left to climb easily on to **Pen y Cyfrwy**, continue around this and drop down towards **Caerfai Bay**.

⑥ You'll eventually come out beneath the Caerfai Bay car park where you turn left on to the road. Follow this past the **Diving Centre** to **St David's** and the start of the walk.

WHILE YOU'RE THERE ℹ
St David's Cathedral is both architecturally stunning and spiritually moving. In 1120 Pope Calixtus II decreed that two pilgrimages to St David's were the equivalent of one to Rome – an honour indeed. The cathedral and the nearby Bishop's Palace play host to a series of classical concerts every summer.

WHAT TO LOOK FOR ℹ
Shortly after the stiff climb out of Porth Clais, you'll round **Trwyn Cynddeiriog**, the headland that divides Porth y Ffynnon from St Non's Bay. This is where St Non and Sant, St David's parents, were said to have lived. A short distance further along the coast path, at the head of the bay, you'll see a footpath on the left that leads to the ruined chapel. This is thought to have been built in the 13th century on the spot where St David was born. A path then leads to a gate, behind which you'll see **St Non's Well** and a grotto. Further up the hill is the newer chapel, dedicated to Our Lady and St Non. This was actually built in the 1930s using stone from other principle local evangelical sites, including the original chapel.

A Revolting Queen at Caistor St Edmund

Walk in the footsteps of Queen Boudica as you explore the countryside around a Roman fortress.

•DISTANCE•	6¼ miles (10km)
•MINIMUM TIME•	3hrs
•ASCENT / GRADIENT•	279ft (85m) ▲▲▲
•LEVEL OF DIFFICULTY•	🚶 🚶 🚶
•PATHS•	Paved road and public footpaths, several sets of steps
•LANDSCAPE•	Rolling farmland and an archaeological site
•SUGGESTED MAP•	aqua3 OS Explorer 237 Norwich
•START / FINISH•	Grid reference: TG 232032
•DOG FRIENDLINESS•	Dogs must be on leads in Roman town
•PARKING•	South Norfolk Council and Norfolk Archaeological Trust car park at Roman fort (free)
•PUBLIC TOILETS•	None on route

BACKGROUND TO THE WALK

When the Romans invaded Britain, they built arrow-straight roads, established well-run, prosperous towns and developed industries like tile-making, salt and potteries. But not all local tribes were pleased to be part of the Roman Empire.

Rebel Queen

One rebel was Boudica, who had been married to King Prasutagus of the Iceni. The trouble started when Prasutagus died in AD 60. He was barely cold in his grave before the Roman procurator's men arrived to grab property and money, and troops appeared to impose military law. One Roman insulted Boudica, who responded with anger, and in retaliation was flogged and her daughters raped. News of this outrage spread like wildfire throughout East Anglia and the revolt was born. Her headquarters are said to have been at or near Venta Icenorum at Caistor.

Fiery Speeches

Contemporary accounts tell us that Boudica was tall, with fierce eyes and a strident voice. She had a mane of tawny hair that tumbled to her waist and she wore a striking multi-coloured tunic, a gold neck torc and a cloak held by a brooch. Female rulers were not unknown to the Iceni and they quickly rallied to her fiery speeches of rebellion and revenge. Other tribes joined the throng as Boudica's army moved against the Romans, carrying huge shields and wearing their best battle gear.

Retaliation

From Venta Icenorum to Colchester they marched, probably using the recently completed Roman road. The army grew until it was said to be 100,000 strong, all angry and determined to exact revenge on their hated oppressors. Meanwhile, Colchester was wholly unprepared for the attack, because the civilians had been assured there was nothing to worry about – they had well-trained Roman soldiers to defend them. But as soon as the garrison spotted the enormous, vengeful throng, they abandoned their posts and fled for safety inside the temple of Claudius. The civilians were left to fend for themselves. A massacre followed of the most shocking magnitude. No one was spared and as many as 20,000 were killed. The wooden town was burned to the ground and the stone temple fell two days later. Boudica then moved on London and St Albans, where the grisly process was repeated.

The Roman general Suetonius marched to meet her and the two forces met near St Albans. Suetonius' well-trained military machine was outnumbered by the Britons, but reports say that the Romans destroyed 80,000 of the larger force – an appalling number of dead for any battle. Boudica probably poisoned herself after the defeat, but her legend lives on. This walk takes you through the lands she once ruled, some of it along the 38-mile (61km) footpath named in her honour.

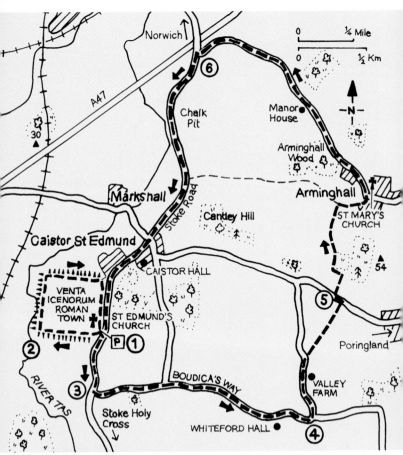

Walk 28 **Directions**

① The first part of the walk follows the marked circular trail around

Venta Icenorum, so go through the gate next to the notice board at the car park. The trail is marked by red and white circles. Climb 36 steps, then go down six to reach the huge bank that protected the town, with a deep ditch to your left. Head west, towards the **River Tas**.

② Turn right by the bench, past fragments of the old walls, and then turn right again when you reach a longer section of wall, still following the trail markers. Go through a gate, then walk along the side of the bank with more wall to your right. Go up 39 steps, then descend again to the ditch on the eastern edge of the town. Go past 11th-century **St Edmund's Church** and when you reach the car park, go through it on to the lane and turn right. You are now on **Boudica's Way**.

WHILE YOU'RE THERE ⓘ

You can see the outskirts of Norwich on parts of this walk, and Norfolk's capital city has a vast amount to offer the visitor, from fine medieval buildings to modern art. The **City of Norwich Aviation Museum** lies 3 miles (4.8km) north of the city, while in the city itself the **Forum** building on Millennium Plain offers an interactive journey through time. Don't miss **Inspire**, a hands-on science discovery exhibition, and the **Sainsbury Centre for Visual Arts**.

---

③ Just after the brick cottages take the tiny unmarked lane to your left, still following Boudica's Way. Go up a hill, keep straight at the next junction and keep walking until you see **Whiteford Hall**.

④ Turn left up **Valley Farm Lane**, following the yellow Boudica's Way markers. After the farm, look for the footpath sign to your right. Take this and keep to your right, along the side of a hedge. Jig right, then immediately left and keep walking until you reach a paved lane. Turn left and then look for another footpath sign to your right.

WHAT TO LOOK FOR ⓘ

Information boards around Venta Icenorum will explain what is what as you walk the perimeter, so look out for them. The **wild flowers** here are also worth seeking out. Between June and September look for common knapweed, which has hairy pink flowers and was once used as a remedy for sore throats. Common mallows are also pink, have a thick, round stem, and large reddish-mauve flowers. Also look for viper's bugloss, a member of the borage family, which has spiky, purplish-violet flowers.

---

⑤ Take the footpath, and follow the markers down a hill and up the other side. It's important to keep to the footpaths here, because there are plenty of signs indicating private property. At the top of the field, take the right-hand path signed towards Arminghall. This narrow track leads you past several houses until you eventually meet a paved lane by **St Mary's Church**, Arminghall. This lane is used by cyclists, so beware. Follow it for about 1¼ miles (2km), using the intermittent gravel track on the left.

⑥ At the T-junction go left, using the gravel path and the verges. Descend a hill into the village of **Caistor St Edmund**, and follow signs for the Roman town, passing 17th-century **Caistor Hall** to your left. Keep walking until you reach the signs for Venta Icenorum, then turn right into the car park.

WHERE TO EAT AND DRINK ⓘ

The **Wildebeest Arms** in nearby Stoke Holy Cross has a family restaurant and offers bar meals as well as selling official leaflets about the Roman site. It has an attractive seating area outside. The Stoke Holy Cross **post office** also sells information leaflets, and a selection of drinks and confectionery.

Bardney's Saintly Paths

An enigmatic outing to the ruined abbeys around Bardney, east of Lincoln.

Walk 29

•DISTANCE•	7¾ miles (12.5km)
•MINIMUM TIME•	4hrs
•ASCENT / GRADIENT•	Negligible
•LEVEL OF DIFFICULTY•	
•PATHS•	Easy field paths and bridleways
•LANDSCAPE•	Flat and open arable land, punctuated by woodland
•SUGGESTED MAP•	aqua3 OS Explorer 273 Lincolnshire Wolds South
•START / FINISH•	Grid reference: TF 120694
•DOG FRIENDLINESS•	Mostly good, watch for livestock
•PARKING•	Horncastle Road, centre of Bardney
•PUBLIC TOILETS•	None on route (nearest at Woodhall Spa)

BACKGROUND TO THE WALK

The gentle valley of the River Witham, east of Lincoln, has long been a fertile place, and for more than just potatoes and sugar beet. Once upon a time it housed as many as nine separate monasteries or religious houses, virtually in sight of one another, attracted by the accessibility that the river afforded as well as the ecclesiastical standing of nearby Lincoln.

The first to be built was Bardney, endowed by Ethelred, King of Mercia, and its fame and popularity was sealed when it became the shrine to St Oswald. King Oswald was killed in battle in AD 642 and his body was brought to Bardney – even though his head went separately to Lindisfarne and his arms to Bamburgh. According to the story, Oswald's remains arrived at night, and the monks at Bardney initially refused to allow the cart to enter. Suddenly a 'pillar of light' shone skywards from the coffin, convincing them that this was indeed a saintly person, and after that they never shut their gates. The local Lincolnshire saying for when someone leaves a door open is: 'Do you come from Bardney?'

Whereas the Benedictine monks of Bardney wore black habits, the Premonstratensian monks (from Premontre, in France) at Tupholme Abbey, which is also visited on this walk, wore a white habit and cap and were known as the 'White Canons'. From Matins at 2AM through to Compline at dusk, they spent their days in prayer and recitation, although they also found time to rear sheep and sell wool as well as importing building stone via a canal-link to the nearby River Witham. Beyond the solitary remaining wall of Tupholme Abbey is a moated field where the canons dug their fish ponds.

But like all the other local religious houses, its decline and ruin was swift once the 16th-century Dissolution Act came into force. Before long it was raided for building material and had farm cottages built against it. In 1972 a large open-air pop festival even took place on the site, featuring such big names as the Beach Boys and Rod Stewart! Fortunately, in 1998, the Heritage Trust managed to step in and save what was left.

On the edge of Bardney, British Sugar's enormous factory was, in its heyday, a hectic place, operating around the clock from September to February in order to process the millions of tonnes of locally grown sugar beet. The huge silos remain, but the plant, built in 1927, has been scaled down in recent years and now only produces 'liquid sugar' (syrup, treacle, and so on), with the mainstream refining switched to Newark and elsewhere.

Walk 29

Walk 29 Directions

① From the **RAF memorial** opposite Bardney post office, walk along the adjacent **Church Lane**. Just beyond **St Lawrence Church** take the public footpath indicated on the left, which squeezes between two fences and turns right along the end of some gardens. (This path can get a little overgrown in the height of summer, in which case follow the road around to the right, past the Methodist chapel, and then left on to the main road, turning off left at the sign for the Viking Way.)

② At the end of the path turn left on to a wide track through the fields, with the huge sugar factory away to your right. Ignore the inviting permissive bridleways into **Southrey Wood** (left).

> **WHERE TO EAT AND DRINK** ⓘ
> The **Black Horse** pub and licensed tea room, on Wragby Road in Bardney, serves all-day meals and light snacks and welcomes walkers. Food is also served daily at **The Bards** ('family pub and restaurant'), also in the centre of Bardney, and at the **Riverside Inn** at Southrey.

③ When the wood finishes continue along the main track, which despite a kink maintains its south easterly direction. When it reaches the buildings of Southrey it swings left past **Poplars Farm**. Take the first road on the right (compare the sight of the old thatched cottage with the modern brick-built village hall next door). At the end of the road go right again to reach the pub at the far end of **Ferry Road**.

④ Turn left on to the raised bank of the **River Witham**. The overgrown platforms and signs of

the former waterside railway station make a strange spectacle, and now you follow the old trackbed alongside the anglers by the river for 650yds (594m).

> **WHAT TO LOOK FOR** ⓘ
> On a neat green in the centre of Bardney, opposite the post office, is an **aviation memorial** featuring a gleaming black propeller. There were airfields dotted across Lincolnshire, of course, but this one commemorates the men of IX Squadron who flew Lancaster bombers out of RAF Bardney between 1943 and 1945. Probably their greatest moment was when they sank the German battleship *Tirpitz* in Norway.

⑤ Go left at a public footpath sign and across a footbridge over a drainage dyke for a track across a field. Continue straight on as it turns into a firmer track and then the surfaced **Campney Lane**.

⑥ At the road junction at the end turn left and, after a sharp left bend, turn right on to a signposted public bridleway. Follow this wide grassy ride between hedges. Go through a gate and past a farm to reach the remains of **Tupholme Abbey**.

⑦ Beyond the abbey turn right on to the road and then almost immediately left on to a quiet lane. About 750yds (686m) after **Low Road Farm** take the public footpath indicated between two fields on the left. The fence is first of all on your right, but when the small dividing dyke appears keep both it and the fence on your left. Go across a small wooden bridge and through another field to turn right on to a cross track all the way to the road.

⑧ Turn left for the verge and then pavement back into **Bardney**.

Skeletons from the Past

Miners tracks to the lead village of Brassington.

•DISTANCE•	5½ miles (9km)
•MINIMUM TIME•	3hrs 30min
•ASCENT / GRADIENT•	1,148ft (350m) ▲ ▲ ▲
•LEVEL OF DIFFICULTY•	🚶 🚶 🚶
•PATHS•	Hill paths, some hard to follow and railway trackbed, numerous stiles
•LANDSCAPE•	Limestone hills
•SUGGESTED MAP•	aqua3 OS Outdoor Leisure 24 White Peak
•START / FINISH•	Grid reference: SK 249528
•DOG FRIENDLINESS•	Dogs on leads over farmland. Can run free on long stretches of enclosed railway trackbed
•PARKING•	Sheepwash pay car park by Carsington Water
•PUBLIC TOILETS•	None on route

BACKGROUND TO THE WALK

'He was as lean as a skeleton, pale as a dead corpse, his hair and beard a deep black, his flesh lank, and, as we thought, something of the colour of lead itself.'

So wrote Daniel Defoe on seeing a lead miner, who had been living in a cave at Harborough Rocks. In times past Carsington and Brassington lived and breathed lead. Prior to the construction of Carsington Water, archaeologists discovered a Romano-British settlement here, which could have been the long-lost Ludutarum, the centre of the lead-mining industry in Roman times.

As you walk out of Carsington into the world of the miner, you're using the very tracks he would have used. But the lesions and pockmarks of the endless excavations are being slowly healed by time, and many wildflowers are beginning to proliferate in the meadows and on hillsides.

Brassington

Weird-shaped limestone crags top the hill, then Brassington appears in the next valley with its Norman church tower rising above the grey rooftops of its 17th- and 18th-century houses. Brassington's post office used to be the tollhouse for the Loughborough turnpike.

St James Church is largely Norman, though it was heavily restored in the late 19th century, including the north aisle, which was added in 1880. The impressive south arcade has fine Perpendicular windows. High on the inner walls of the Norman tower is a figure of a man with his hand on his heart. The carving is believed to be Saxon: the man, Brassington's oldest resident.

Climbing out of Brassington the route takes you over Hipley Hill, where there are more remnants of the mines, and more fascinating limestone outcrops. On the top you could have caught the train back, but the Cromford High Peak railway closed in 1967, so you are left with a walk along its trackbed. It's a pleasant walk though, through a wooded cutting, with meadow cranesbill and herb Robert thriving among trackside verges and crags: there are even raspberries at one point.

Harborough Rocks beckon from the left. Archaeologists have uncovered evidence that sabre-toothed tigers, black bears and hyenas once sought the shelter of nearby caves. They also discovered relics and artefacts from Roman and Iron Age dwellers. For those with extra time, there's an entertaining path winding between the popular climbing crags to the summit, which gives wide views across the White Peak and the lowlands of the East Midlands. Carsington Water is seen to perfection, surrounded by chequered fields, woods and low rounded hills.

Leaving the railway behind, there's one last hill, Carsington Pasture, to descend before returning to the lake. Last time I was there they were racing Land Rovers and Jeeps across the tops so you might get some added entertainment.

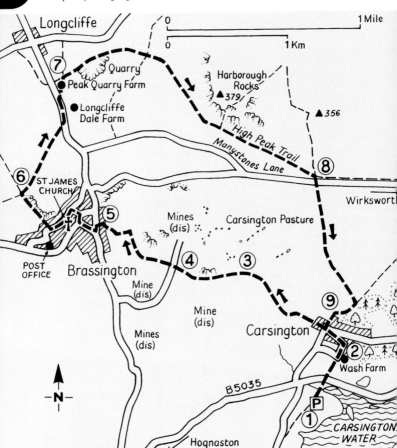

Walk 30 Directions

① Take the signposted path northwards towards **Carsington**. It winds through scrub woods and rounds a finger of the lake before reaching the B5035 road. The path continues on the other side, meeting a lane by **Wash Farm** and following it to enter the village by the **Miners Arms**.

Walk 30

②Turn left along the lane to reach the **Hopton road**. Where the road turns left go straight ahead along a narrow lane passing several cottages. Beyond a gate the lane becomes a fine green track beneath the limestone-studded slopes of **Carsington Pasture**.

③ Where the track swings left you reach a gate; go through then immediately fork right off the main path on a path climbing the grassy slopes to the west. At the top aim right of a copse and go through a gap in the broken wall before descending into a little valley.

> **WHERE TO EAT AND DRINK** ⓘ
> You can break the route for refreshment at the ivy-clad **Ye Old Gate Inn**, which serves Marstons ales. Children must be ten years old or over.

④ Go over two stiles to cross a country lane, then follow a miners' track for 200yds (183m) towards some old mine workings. Here a footpath sign directs you around some limestone outcrops before arcing right towards **Brassington**. Turn left at the footpath signpost and follow the waymarked route across the fields into the village.

⑤ Turn left, then immediately right up **Miners Hill**. Now go right up **Jasper Lane**, left up **Red Lion Hill**, and left again along **Hillside Lane**. After 200yds (183m) leave the lane for a footpath on the right, which climbs past more limestone outcrops. The faint waymarked path gradually veers right, and passes the head of a green lane.

⑥ Here climb right to a waymarking post. Through the next three fields the path climbs parallel to, and to the right of, a line of

> **WHILE YOU'RE THERE** ⓘ
> Take a look round nearby **Hognaston**, which is an ancient Norse settlement dominated by its fine church dedicated to St Bartholomew. The church dates back to 1200 and has an ornate Norman doorway with a tympanium showing a bishop and his crook, with lambs and wild beasts. In medieval times the church tower with its 5ft (1.5m) thick walls was used as a keep to protect villagers' livestock.

wooden electricity pylons. In the fourth field bear half right above the rock outcrops and go through the top gate. Now aim for the extensive buildings of **Longcliffe Dale Farm**. After going over the next stile, turn left up the road, passing the farm. A footpath on the right then cuts a corner to the **High Peak Trail**, passing an electricity sub station and **Peak Quarry Farm**.

⑦ Turn right along the trackbed of the **High Peak Trail** passing the **Harborough Rocks**.

⑧ Go right at the footpath signed to **Carsington**. This descends a small field to cross **Manystones Lane**. Follow the wall across **Carsington Pasture**, then descend by woods to a gate by a cottage.

⑨ Turn left down a little ginnel leading to the road and left again to retrace your earlier route back to **Sheepwash** car park.

> **WHAT TO LOOK FOR** ⓘ
> Despite their apparently sterile soil, the old mine spoil tips have been colonised by a range of adaptable lead tolerant plants, flourishing among the grassy heaps. You may well see the mountain pansy, the spring sandwort, eyebright or autumn gentians, adding a new colourful complexion to the hillside.

Cromford and the Black Rocks

Walk through the Industrial Revolution in a valley where history was made.

•**DISTANCE**•	5 miles (8km)
•**MINIMUM TIME**•	3hrs
•**ASCENT / GRADIENT**•	720ft (220m) ▲ ▲ ▲
•**LEVEL OF DIFFICULTY**•	🚶 🚶 🚶
•**PATHS**•	Well-graded – canal tow paths, lanes, forest paths and a railway trackbed, quite a few stiles
•**LANDSCAPE**•	Town streets and wooded hillsides
•**SUGGESTED MAP**•	aqua3 OS Explorer OL24 White Peak
•**START / FINISH**•	Grid reference: SK 300571
•**DOG FRIENDLINESS**•	Dogs on leads over farmland, can run free on long stretches of enclosed railway trackbed
•**PARKING**•	Cromford Wharf pay car park
•**PUBLIC TOILETS**•	At car park

BACKGROUND TO THE WALK

For many centuries Cromford, 'the ford by the bend in the river', was no more than a sleepy backwater. Lead mining brought the village brief prosperity, but by the 18th century even that was in decline. Everything changed in 1771 when Sir Richard Arkwright decided to build the world's first watered-powered cotton-spinning mill here. Within 20 years he had built two more, and had constructed a whole new town around them. Cromford was awake to the Industrial Revolution and would be connected to the rest of Britain by a network of roads, railways and canals.

As you walk through the cobbled courtyard of the Arkwright Mill, now being restored by the Arkwright Society, you are transported back into that austere world of the 18th century, back to the times when mother, father and children all worked at the mills.

Most of the town lies on the other side of the busy A6, including the mill pond which was built by Arkwright to impound the waters of Bonsall Brook, and the beautifully restored mill workers' cottages of North Street.

The Black Rocks

The Black Rocks overlook the town from the south. The walk makes a beeline for them through little ginnels, past some almshouses and through pine woods. You'll see climbers grappling with the 80ft (24m) gritstone crags, but there's a good path all the way to the top. Here you can look across the Derwent Valley to the gaunt skeleton of Riber Castle, to the beacon on top of Crich Stand and down the Derwent Gorge to Matlock.

The Cromford and High Peak Railway

The next stage of the journey takes you on to the High Peak Trail, which uses the former trackbed of the Cromford and High Peak Railway. Engineered by Josias Jessop, and built in the 1830s the railway was built as an extension of the canal system and, as such, the stations were called wharfs. In the early years horses pulled the wagons on the level stretches, while steam-winding engines worked the inclines. By the mid-1800s steam engines worked the whole line, which connected with the newly-extended Midland Railway. The railway was closed by Dr Beeching in 1967.

The Canal

After abandoning the High Peak Trail pleasant forest paths lead you down into the valley at High Peak Junction, where the old railway met the Cromford Canal. The 33-mile (53.5km) canal was built in 1793, a year after Arkwright's death, to link up with the Erewash, thus completing a navigable waterway to the River Trent at Trent Lock. Today, there's an information centre here, a fascinating place to muse before that final sojourn along the tow path to Cromford.

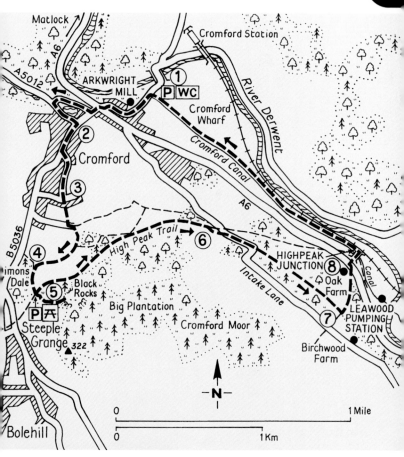

Walk 31 Directions

① Turn left out of the car park on to **Mill Road**. Cross the A6 to the **Market Place**. Turn right down the **Scarthin**, passing the **Boat Inn** and the old millpond before doubling back left along **Water Lane** to **Cromford Hill**.

② Turn right, past the shops and

Bell Inn, then turn left up **Bedehouse Lane,** which turns into a narrow tarmac ginnel after rounding some almshouses (otherwise known as bedehouses).

③ At the top of the lane by a street of 1970s housing, a signpost for **Black Rocks** points uphill. The footpath continues its climb southwards to meet a lane. Turn left along the winding lane, which soon divides. Take the right fork, a limestone track leading to a stone-built house with woods behind. On reaching the house, turn right through a gate, and follow the top field edge.

④ After climbing some steps, ascend left through the woods of **Dimons Dale** up to the **Black Rocks** car park and picnic site. The track you've reached is on the former trackbed of the **Cromford and High Peak Railway.** Immediately opposite is the there-and-back waymarked detour leading to the rocks.

⑤ Returning to the car park, turn right along the **High Peak Trail,** which traverses the hillside high above **Cromford.**

⑥ After about ¾ mile (1.2km) watch out for a path on the right leaving the Trail for **Intake Lane.** On reaching the lane, turn right and follow it to a sharp left-hand bend. Here, go straight on,

> **WHAT TO LOOK FOR**   ⓘ
> Besides the Arkwright Mill, which is a 'must see' venue, take some time to visit the exhibits in old railway workshops at High Peak Junction and the Leawood Pumping Station, which pumped water from the River Derwent to the Cromford Canal. The restored Leawood works has a working Cornish-type beam engine.

following a path heading south east along the top edge of some woodland. (**Note:** Neither the path nor the wood is shown on the current Ordnance Survey Explorer OL map of the White Peak.)

⑦ On nearing **Birchwood Farm,** watch out for two paths coming up from the left. Take the one descending more directly downhill (north west, then north). At the bottom of the woods the path swings left across fields, coming out to the A6 road by **Oak Farm.**

⑧ Cross the road and follow the little ginnel opposite, over the **Matlock railway** and the **Cromford Canal.** Go past the **High Peak Junction** information centre, then turn left along the canal tow path. Follow this back to the car park at **Cromford Wharf.**

> **WHERE TO EAT AND DRINK**   ⓘ
> **Arkwright's Mill** has a small café for coffee, cake and light snacks. For bar meals try the **Greyhound Inn** at Cromford. The excellent **Boat Inn** free house on the Scarthin at Cromford serves bar meals at lunchtime only.

> **WHILE YOU'RE THERE**   ⓘ
> If you have time, visit **Wirksworth,** a former lead mining town on the hillsides above Cromford. Until a restoration project of the 1980s Wirksworth had become a dusty, derelict place that nobody wanted to visit. Take a look at the **National Stone Centre** on Portway Lane. Here you can have a go at gem panning and join guided walks. The **Wirksworth Heritage Centre,** which is housed in a former silk and velvet mill at Crown Yard, gives a fascinating insight into the town's history.

Conwy: Castle High and Castle Low

Conwy's magnificent castle lies at the foot of the Carneddau, but up there in the foothills there's a remote fort, an outpost of the Celtic era.

Walk 32

•DISTANCE•	6½ miles (10.4km)
•MINIMUM TIME•	4hrs
•ASCENT / GRADIENT•	1,214ft (370m) ▲▲▲
•LEVEL OF DIFFICULTY•	🚶 🚶 🚶
•PATHS•	Good paths and easy-to-follow moorland tracks, 6 stiles
•LANDSCAPE•	Town, coastline high ridge, farmland and copse
•SUGGESTED MAP•	aqua3 OS Explorer OL17 Snowdon
•START / FINISH•	Grid reference: SH 782776
•DOG FRIENDLINESS•	OK on high ridges, but keep on leads elsewhere
•PARKING•	Large car park on Llanrwst Road behind Conwy Castle
•PUBLIC TOILETS•	At car park

BACKGROUND TO THE WALK

Conwy is special. Approaching from Llandudno Junction, three fine bridges (including Thomas Telford's magnificent suspension bridge of 1822) cross the estuary beneath the mighty castle, allowing the road and the railway into this medieval World Heritage Site. The fortress dates back to 1287, when the powerful English King Edward I built it as part of his 'iron ring' to repress the rebellious troops of Llewelyn the Great, who had given him a great deal of trouble in his conquest of Wales.

Great town walls with gates and towers still encircle old Conwy. You should walk these walls, for they offer a fine rooftop view of the castle, the Conwy Estuary and the rocky knolls of Deganwy, before you arrive at the quayside where you can watch the fishermen sorting their nets and the seagulls watching out for any scraps. The walk description begins at the quayside, not the car park, as you will probably want to take a good look around this medieval town. The route starts on a shoreline path under the boughs of Bondlobeb Wood.

The Ancient Settlements of Conwy Mountain

Not long after passing through Conwy's suburbs you're walking the hillside, on a path threading through gorse and small wind-twisted hawthorns. If you liked the views from the castle walls, you'll love the view from the Conwy Mountain ridge. Looking back, you can see the castle, towering over the town's roof tops; but now added to the scene are the Carneddau, the limestone isthmus of the Great Orme and, across the great sands of Lafan, Anglesey.

There is quite a network of paths criss-crossing the ridge and usually the best course is the highest: you'll need to be on the crest path to see the remains of Castell Caer. This 10-acre (4ha) fort has been linked to both Roman and Iron-Age settlers – it certainly has formidable defences, with clearly visible artificial ramparts that overlook spectacular sea cliffs on one side, and a wide view of the land to the south. Beyond the fort, the path misses out the peaks of Penmaen-bach and Alltwen, which is just as well, for the former has been heavily quarried for its roadstone – you probably drove over some of it on your way up the motorway. Instead you should descend to the Sychnant Pass, a splendid, twisting gorge that separates Conwy Mountain from the higher Carneddau peaks.

It's all downhill from here, but the scenery becomes more varied and still maintains interest. As you descend you can see the tidal River Conwy, twisting amongst chequered green fields. Little hills present themselves to you, on your way back north. One last one has pleasant woods with primroses and bluebells, and it gives you another fine view of Conwy Castle to add to your collection before returning to base.

Walk 32 Directions

① From **Conwy Quay** head north west along the waterfront, past the

Smallest House and under the town walls. Fork right along a tarmac waterside footpath that rounds **Bodlondeb Wood**. Turn left along the road, past the school and

Walk 32

on to the **A547**. Cross the road, then the railway line by a footbridge. The lane beyond skirts a wood to reach another lane, where you turn right.

② Another waymarker guides you on to a footpath on the right that, beyond a stile, rakes up wooded hillsides up on to **Conwy Mountain**. Follow the undulating crest of Conwy Mountain past **Castell Caer**.

③ Several tracks converge in the high fields of **Pen-pyra**. Here, follow signposts for the North Wales Path along the track heading to the south west over the left shoulder of **Alltwen** and down to the metalled road traversing the **Sychnant Pass**.

④ Follow the footpath from the other side of the road, skirting the

woods on your left. Pass **Gwern Engen** on your left-hand side and continue to pass to the left of the **Lodge**, to reach a lane. Turn right along the lane, then turn left, when you reach the next junction, into **Groesffordd** village. Cross the road, then take the road ahead that swings to the right past a telephone box, then left (south east) towards **Plas Iolyn**.

⑤ Turn left at the next junction, then right at a signposted enclosed footpath that crosses fields all the way to the **B5106**. Turn left along this, then right when you get to the entrance to a caravan park, following frequent waymarkers through scrubland and scaling several stiles. After crossing a surfaced vehicle track, and descending into a little hollow, the path climbs left (north) along a pastured ridge, with a telephone mast straight ahead.

⑥ Turn left along the road you have now encountered then go right to pass to the right-hand side of the telephone mast and **Bryn-Iocyn farm**. On reaching **Coed Benarth wood**, turn left then follow the narrow path northwards through the woods.

⑦ Go over a ladder stile on your left-hand side and descend a field to a roadside gate at the bottom. Turn right on to the **B5106** to return to the quayside, or turn left to get back to the main car park.

Wizardly Wanderings at Alderley Edge

Layers of history and legend surrounding this famous Cheshire landmark make this short walk a rich mixture.

•DISTANCE•	3 miles (4.8km)
•MINIMUM TIME•	1hr
•ASCENT / GRADIENT•	445ft (136m) ▲▲▲
•LEVEL OF DIFFICULTY•	👥 👥 👥
•PATHS•	Woodland tracks and paths, some field paths, 7 stiles
•LANDSCAPE•	Woodland, scattered sandstone crags, some farmland
•SUGGESTED MAP•	aqua3 OS Explorer 268 Wilmslow, Macclesfield & Congleton
•START / FINISH•	Grid reference: SJ 860772
•DOG FRIENDLINESS•	On lead on farmland and always under close control
•PARKING•	Large National Trust car park off B5087
•PUBLIC TOILETS•	At car park

BACKGROUND TO THE WALK

There's a lot to take in at Alderley Edge, on the ground, under the ground and even – many believe – in other dimensions entirely.

Ancient Mines and Legends

As long as 4,000 years ago, there was mining activity here, using tools of wood and stone. Mining went on through Roman times but reached its greatest intensity in the 19th century. Copper and lead were the main products, though various other ores were also worked.

Alderley Edge is as rich in legend as it is in minerals. In fact it is probably true that it is rich in legend because of its long history of exploitation. Old shafts and levels or overgrown heaps of spoil can mystify later generations and inspire speculation. Also, working underground, especially in the fickle light of tallow candles or primitive lamps, seems to stimulate the imagination. Waves of immigration, such as those of Cornish miners, import new layers of legend, too.

A Hidden Cave

The most famous legend of the area is alluded to in the names of the Wizard Inn and Wizard's Well, both passed on this walk. Hidden somewhere on the Edge is a cave, guarded by a wizard, in which an army of men and horses sleeps, ready to emerge and save the country when the need is dire. No one has found this cave (though it must be a big one) but you can see the wizard, or at least an effigy, carved in the rocks above the Wizard's Well.

Air of Mystery

This story, and the general air of mystery which often pervades the edge, especially on a misty day with few people about, have inspired many of the books of local author Alan Garner, of which the best known is *The Weirdstone of Brisingamen* (1960).

The walk itself is largely through woodland. In fact the wooded aspect of Alderley Edge is relatively recent. The demand for fuel, building timber and pit props ensured that the area was cleared of its trees from the Bronze Age onwards. The local landowner, Lord Stanley, began extensive plantings in the mid-18th century and today the National Trust manage the woodlands carefully. Although the Edge is elevated above the surrounding countryside, its wooded nature means that distant views are rarely unobstructed. From the crest of Castle Rock there is a broad window to the north, towards Manchester with the hills of Lancashire beyond, while at Stormy Point the view opens to the east, towards the Peak District.

There are exceptions to the woodland rule. Behind Sand Hills, in the earlier part of the walk, there are damp areas with many orchids, and pools fringed by yellow iris and reed mace (the tall club-headed reed often wrongly called the bulrush). Nearing the end, there's some open farmland.

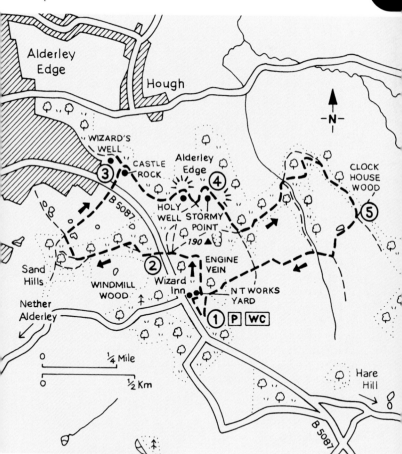

Walk 33 Directions

① From the large National Trust car park, just off the B5087, walk towards the tea room and information room. Go right on a wide track past the National Trust works yard, then left. Cross an open area past **Engine Vein**. At a crossroads of paths turn left and come out by **Beacon Lodge**.

Walk 33

② Go straight across the road into **Windmill Wood**. Follow a gently descending track to a clearing, bear left and continue descending. About 140yds (128m) beyond a National Trust sign, in more open terrain now, with bare sand hills ahead of you, bear right across the grass to a crossroads with a field ahead. Turn right, skirting around some damp ground and then a pool. Just before another open field, go right, along the edge of the wood. Continue in a narrow strip of trees, with fields either side. Cross the road again and follow a track to the bare crest of **Castle Rock**.

WHAT TO LOOK FOR
Signs of **mining activity** can be seen in many places, most noticeably at Engine Vein and Stormy Point. There are deep covered shafts within the open working of Engine Vein. Most of what you see today was excavated in the 18th century, but there is evidence of much earlier working. The exposure of bare rock at Stormy Point is partly due to toxic minerals, though wear and tear by the feet of visitors plays a part too.

③ Descend the steps to a level path. Go left 120yds (110m) to **Wizard's Well**. Return to the steps and continue below the crags on a terrace path, then up steps to join a higher path. Go left and almost immediately start descending again, with more steps in places. At the bottom cross a footbridge and climb again, levelling out briefly by the **Holy Well**. A few paces to its left

go up over tree roots to where the path resumes. Climb shallow steps to a wider path, go left then turn right on to the rocky crest of **Stormy Point**.

WHERE TO EAT AND DRINK
The **Wizard tea room**, open 1–5PM weekends and bank holidays, serves great cakes. The adjacent **Wizard Inn** is really a smart restaurant. For normal pub service, including decent beer and a good range of meals, there's the **Royal Oak** on Heyes Lane down in Alderley Edge village.

④ Follow the wide level track to a crossroads and go left. Follow signs 'Hare Hill', down a steady descent with a small ravine at the bottom. Turn right and ascend again. Climb steps past tall beech trees, then descend through **Clock House Wood**. Climb again to a National Trust sign and out into the open.

⑤ Go right, over a stile, across the waist of a field to another stile near a pond. Go left along the hedge to a stile hidden in a curve, then up a fenced path. Join a wider track and at the top and go over a stile on the right. Go left over the next stile and up to another stile and grassy track. Cross a gravel track into another narrow fenced path and at its end turn left. Opposite the National Trust works yard you can go left through a gate for a shortcut to the car park or continue straight on to the tea room.

WHILE YOU'RE THERE
There's a working **watermill** at Nether Alderley. The building dates from the 15th century though most of the machinery is more recent. It's also a chance to find out exactly why Millstone Grit is so called. The walled gardens and surrounding park of **Hare Hill**, probably best known for azaleas and rhododendrons, can be reached by a longer walk from Alderley Edge. About 2 miles (3.2km) away, it's fairly well signposted. The gardens are cared for by the National Trust.

Marching Roads and Battlefields

Following the ancient roads over Win Hill to the Roman Fort at Navio, via the site of an ancient battle.

•DISTANCE•	8¾ miles (14km)
•MINIMUM TIME•	5hrs
•ASCENT / GRADIENT•	1,050ft (320m) ▲▲▲
•LEVEL OF DIFFICULTY•	🚶🚶 🚶🚶 🚶
•PATHS•	Paths can be slippery after rain, quite a few stiles
•LANDSCAPE•	Riverside pastureland and high peak
•SUGGESTED MAP•	aqua3 OS Outdoor Leisure 1 Dark Peak
•START / FINISH•	Grid reference: SK 149829
•DOG FRIENDLINESS•	Dogs should be kept on leads, except on high fell
•PARKING•	Main Castleton pay car park
•PUBLIC TOILETS•	At car park

BACKGROUND TO THE WALK

Leaving Castleton beneath Peveril Castle's Norman keep sets the scene for a walk through history. You're treading the same ground as Roman soldiers and Celtic and Saxon warriors before you.

The walk takes you onto the hillside beyond the sycamores of the River Noe. As you amble across green pastures overlooking the Hope Valley, cast your imagination back to the dark days of AD 926. Down there in the valley below you, a furious tribal battle ended in victory for King Athelstan, grandson of Alfred the Great. He would soon become the first Saxon ruler of all England.

Navio: A Roman Fort

In one of those riverside fields the path comes across the earthwork remains of the Roman fort, Navio. Built in the time of Emperor Antoninus Pius, the fort stood at a junction of roads serving garrisons at Buxton, Glossop, and Templeborough. At its peak it would have sheltered over 500 soldiers. It remained occupied until the 4th century, controlling the rich mining area around the Peak. Many Roman relics found near the fort can be viewed at the Buxton Museum.

Win Hill looms large in your thoughts as you cross to the other side of the valley and climb towards it. As you're passing through the hamlet of Aston take a quick look at Aston Hall. Built in 1578, it has an unusual pedimented window with a weather-worn carved figure. The doorway is surrounded by Roman Doric columns and a four-centred arch.

Beyond the hall the climb begins in earnest up a stony track, then through bracken and grass hillside where Win Hill's rocky summit peeps out across the heathered ridge. A concrete trig point caps the rocks. And what a view to reward your efforts! The Ladybower Reservoir's sinuous shorelines creep between dark spruce woods, while the gritstone tors of Kinder Scout, the Derwent Edge, and Bleaklow fill the northern horizon, framed by the pyramidal Lose Hill.

There are several theories on how Win Hill got its name. The most likely one is that it derives from an earlier name, Wythinehull, which meant Willow Hill. The best theory though concerns two warlords, Edwin, the first Christian king of Northumbria, and Cuicholm, King of Wessex. Cuicholm murdered Lilla, Edwin's maidservant, and Edwin was looking for revenge. Cuicholm assembled his forces on Lose Hill, while his enemy camped on Win Hill. Edwin, was victorious and thus his hill was named Win Hill. Now you follow Edwin down the hill, before continuing across the Hope Valley fields back to Castleton.

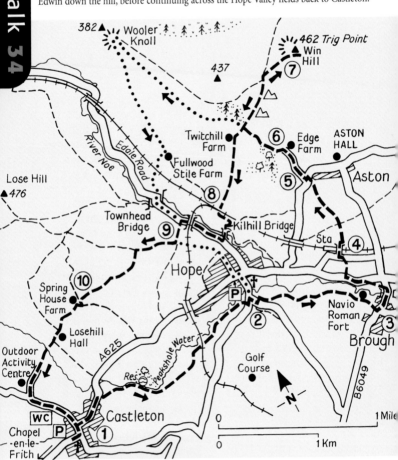

Walk 34 Directions

① Turn left out of the car park along the main street. At the far end of the village turn right on a walled stony lane and continue along a well-defined path accompanying **Peakhole Water**. Cross the railway with care and continue along the path to its end at **Pindale Road**.

② Turn left here, then right at the next junction. After about 100yds (91m), go over a stile by a gate and follow the path running roughly parallel to the lane at first, then the **River Noe**, to reach the site of the Roman fort of **Navio**. Beyond the earthworks go over a stile in a fence and bear half right across another field to reach the B6409 road at **Brough**.

Walk 34

③ Turn left through the village and cross the footbridge over the **River Noe**. Go left over a stile and head north west to the A625. Turn left along the road for 200yds (183m) to a small gate just beyond a cottage. Follow the hedge and dyke on the right to pass to the right of some houses.

> **WHAT TO LOOK FOR** ⓘ
>
> Hope is on the edge of limestone country. Often you can see the change in the dry-stone walls. Those in the valley are made from paler limestone, while those on the Win Hill slopes are of the darker gritstone. These walls were mostly built between 1780 and 1820, when enclosure of upland areas was taking place at a prolific rate right across the country. Although expensive to build and repair, they're are now considered to be an integral part of the Peakland landscape and various conservation bodies devote time to training new generations of skilled wallers.

④ Turn left along the lane towards the railway station, then go right along a narrow path which leads to a footbridge over the line. Cross the bridge and turn right at its far end, then left over a stile to cross yet more fields, this time keeping the fence on your right.

⑤ When you reach **Aston** turn left along the road, then almost immediately turn right along a narrow, surfaced lane, signposted 'To Win Hill'.

> **WHILE YOU'RE THERE** ⓘ
>
> If you're here on August Bank Holiday Monday you should visit the **Hope Agricultural Show** and sheepdog trials.

⑥ Beyond **Edge Farm** an unsurfaced track on the left takes the route along the top edge of some woods to a path junction above **Twitchill Farm**. Now climb right on a well-used path to **Win Hill**'s summit.

⑦ From the summit retrace your steps back to the junction above **Twitchill Farm**. This time descend left past the Farm, to the railway.

⑧ Turn left under the railway tunnel, where the lane doubles back left and winds its way to **Kilhill Bridge**, then the **Edale Road**. Turn right along the road, under the railway bridge, then turn left on a field path.

⑨ By a cottage turn right on a path climbing towards **Lose Hill**. Take the left fork at a signposted junction of paths to follow a waymarked route westwards to **Spring House Farm**.

⑩ Beyond the farmhouse, turn right along a stony track heading west behind **Losehill Hall**. Where the lane swings left, leave it to follow a cross-field path, which joins an unsurfaced lane. After passing the outdoor activity centre, turn left along **Hollowford Road**, back into **Castleton**.

> **WHERE TO EAT AND DRINK** ⓘ
>
> The **Castle** in Castle Street serves Bass beer and good bar meals. Closer to hand you could seek out the **Woodbine Café** in Hope which serves pies, bacon sandwiches and hot drinks.

Walk 35

Bradfield and the Dale Dike Dam Disaster

A quiet waterside walk around the site of a horrific 19th-century industrial tragedy.

•DISTANCE•	5½ miles (9km)
•MINIMUM TIME•	3hrs 30min
•ASCENT / GRADIENT•	394ft (120m) ▲ ▲ ▲
•LEVEL OF DIFFICULTY•	👫 👫 👫
•PATHS•	Minor roads, bridleways, forest paths
•LANDSCAPE•	Woodland, reservoir and meadows
•SUGGESTED MAP•	aqua3 OS Explorer OL1 Dark Peak
•START / FINISH•	Grid reference: SK 262920
•DOG FRIENDLINESS•	Keep on lead near livestock
•PARKING•	By cricket ground in Bradfield
•PUBLIC TOILETS•	None on route

BACKGROUND TO THE WALK

Just before midnight on Friday 11 March 1864, when the Dale Dike Dam collapsed, 650 million gallons (2,955 million litres) of water surged along the Loxley Valley towards Sheffield, leaving a trail of death and destruction. When the floods finally subsided 244 people had been killed and hundreds of properties destroyed.

The Bradfield Scheme

During the Industrial Revolution Sheffield expanded rapidly, as country people sought employment in the city's steel and cutlery works. This put considerable pressure on the water supply. The 'Bradfield Scheme' was Sheffield Waterworks Company's ambitious proposal to build massive reservoirs in the hills around the village of Bradfield, about 8 miles (12.9km) from the city. Work commenced on the first of these, the Dale Dike Dam on 1 January 1859. It was a giant by the standards of the time with a capacity of over 700 million gallons (3,182 million litres) of water, but some 200 million gallons (910 million litres) less than the present reservoir.

The Disaster of 1864

Construction of the dam continued until late February 1864, by which time the reservoir was almost full. Friday 11 March was a stormy day and as one of the dam workers crossed the earthen embankment on his way home, he noticed a crack, about a finger's width, running along it. John Gunson, the chief engineer, turned out with one of the contractors to inspect the dam. They had to make the 8 miles (12.9km) from Sheffield in a horse-drawn gig, in deteriorating weather conditions, so it was 10PM before they got there. After an initial inspection, Gunson concluded that it was probably nothing to worry about. However as a precaution he decided to lower the water level. He re-inspected the crack at 11:30PM, noting that it had not visibly deteriorated. However, then the engineer saw to his horror that water was running over the top of the embankment into the crack. He was making his way to the bottom of the embankment when he felt the ground beneath him begin to shake and saw the top of the dam breached by the straining waters. He just had time to scramble up the side before a large section of the dam collapsed, unleashing a solid wall of water down into the valley below towards Sheffield. The torrent destroyed everything in its path and though the waters started to subside within half an hour their destructive force swept aside 415 houses, 106 factories or shops, 20 bridges and countless cottage and market gardens for 8 miles (12.9km). Men women and children were not spared, some whole families were wiped out, including an 87-year-old woman and a 2-day-old baby.

At the inquest the jury concluded that there had been insufficient engineering skill devoted to a work of such size and called for legislation to ensure 'frequent, sufficient and regular' inspections of dams. The Dale Dike Dam was rebuilt in 1875 but it was not brought into full use until 1887, a very dry year.

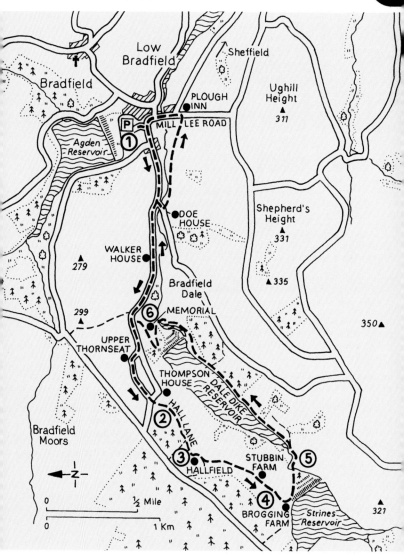

Walk 35 Directions

① Exit the car park and turn right on to the road. At a Y-junction go right towards Midhopestones. Follow this road uphill passing, on the right, a former inn, **Walker House** farm and **Upper Thornseat**. When the road turns sharply right, at the entrance to **Thomson House**, turn left on to the farm road.

② From here go through a gate in front of you and on to **Hall Lane**, a public bridleway. Follow this along the edge of a wood then through another gate and continue right on the farm road. Another gate at the end of this road leads to the entrance to **Hallfield**.

WHERE TO EAT AND DRINK
The **Plough Inn** is over 200 years old and has held a licence for most of that time. A former farmhouse, it contains an enormous stone hearth, stone walls and traditional timbers. Real ales and traditional home-cooked food is the standard fare with a splendid selection of roasts on a Sunday. Children are very welcome if eating.

③ The right of way goes through the grounds of Hallfield but an alternative permissive path leads left over a stile, round the perimeter of the house and across another stile to re-join the bridleway at the back of the house. Follow the bridleway crossing a stile, a gate and then past **Stubbin Farm**.

④ The next gate leads to **Brogging Farm** and the dam at the head of Strines Reservoir. Look out for a sign near the end of the farmhouse and turn left. Go slightly downhill, over a stile, follow the path, then cross a stile and go through a wood.

⑤ Cross the stream by a footbridge, keep to the right, ignoring a second footbridge, then follow the path along the bank of **Dale Dike Reservoir** to the dam head. From here continue through the woods, down several sets of steps and continue on the path looking out for the memorial to those who were killed as a result of the dam breaching in 1864.

WHILE YOU'RE THERE
Don't miss the Parish **Church of St Nicholas,** which dates from 1487. It contains a Norman font gifted by the Cistercian monks at Roche Abbey and a Saxon cross found at Low Bradfield in the late 19th century. But it is the Watch House at the gates of the church that sets it apart. Built in 1745 to prevent body snatching it is the last one to survive in Yorkshire.

⑥ Follow the path until it reaches the road. Cross the stile, turn right on to the road and proceed to the Y-Junction. Turn right, cross the bridge then look for a public footpath sign to Low Bradfield just before the entrance to **Doe House**. Cross the stile on the left and follow the path. The path crosses two stiles then terminates at a T-junction with **Mill Lee Road** opposite the **Plough Inn**. Turn left and follow this road downhill, through the village and back to the car park.

WHAT TO LOOK FOR
A **memorial** was erected at the dam in 1991 to commemorate those who lost their lives in the flood. It's a simple memorial stone surrounded by a small garden. Next to it there's a white stone bearing the letters CLOB. This is one of four stones that mark the Centre Line of the Old Bank and are the only trace today of where the earthen embankment of the previous dam stood.

Halifax and the Shibden Valley

An old packhorse track, a superb half-timbered hall and a hidden valley – all just a short walk from Halifax.

•DISTANCE•	4½ miles (7.2km)
•MINIMUM TIME•	2hrs 30min
•ASCENT / GRADIENT•	410ft (125m) ▲ ▲ ▲
•LEVEL OF DIFFICULTY•	👫 👫 👫
•PATHS•	Old packhorse tracks and field paths, no stiles
•LANDSCAPE•	Surprisingly rural, considering the proximity to Halifax
•SUGGESTED MAP•	aqua3 OS Explorer 288 Bradford & Huddersfield
•START / FINISH•	Grid reference: SE 095254
•DOG FRIENDLINESS•	Keep on lead crossing busy roads
•PARKING•	In Halifax
•PUBLIC TOILETS•	Halifax (near bus station)

BACKGROUND TO THE WALK

Set amongst the Pennine hills, Halifax was a town in the vanguard of the Industrial Revolution. Its splendid civic buildings and huge mills are a good indication of the town's prosperity, won from the woollen trade. Ironically, the most splendid building of all came close to being demolished. The Piece Hall, built in 1779, predates the industrial era. Here, in a total of 315 rooms on three collonaded floors, the hand-weavers of the district would offer their wares (known as 'pieces') for sale to cloth merchants. The collonades surround a massive square. Your first reaction on walking into the square may be surprise, for this is a building that would not look out of place in Renaissance Italy.

The mechanisation of the weaving process left the Piece Hall largely redundant. In the intervening years it has served a variety of purposes, including as a venue for political oration and as a wholesale market. During the 1970s, having narrowly escaped the wrecking ball, the Piece Hall was spruced up and given a new lease of life. Now it houses a museum, tourist information centre and a number of small shops and businesses. But the building's full potential as a tourist attraction has yet to be realised.

The Magna Via

The cobbled thoroughfare that climbs so steeply up Beacon Hill is known as the Magna Via. Until 1741, when a turnpike road was built, this was the only practicable approach to Halifax from the east, for both foot and packhorse traffic. Also known as Wakefield Gate, the Magna Via linked up with the Long Causeway, the old high level road to Burnley. That intrepid 18th-century traveller, Daniel Defoe, was one of those who struggled up this hill. 'We quitted Halifax not without some astonishment at its situation, being so surrounded with hills, and those so high as makes the coming in and going out of it exceedingly troublesome'. The route was superseded in the 1820s by the turnpike constructed through Godley Cutting. Today the Magna Via, too steep to be adopted for modern motor vehicles, remains a fascinating relic of the past.

Shibden Hall

Situated on a hill above Halifax, this magnificent half-timbered house is set in 90 acres (36ha) of beautiful, rolling parkland. Dating from 1420, the hall has been owned by prominent local families – the Oates, Saviles, Waterhouses and, latterly, the Listers. All these families left their mark on the fabric of the house, but, the core of the original house remains intact. The rooms are furnished in period style, to show how they might have looked over almost six centuries. The oak furniture and panelling has that patina of age that antique forgers try in vain to emulate. Barns and other outbuildings have been converted into a folk museum, with displays of old vehicles, tools and farm machinery.

When Emily Brontë created Thrushcross Grange in her only novel *Wuthering Heights*, she may have had Shibden Hall in mind. It certainly proved a suitable location in 1991 for a film version of the famous story, which starred Ralph Fiennes as Heathcliffe and Juliette Binoche as Cathy.

Walk 36 **Directions**

① Walk downhill, past a tall spire that once belonged to **Square**

Church, and down **Church Street**, passing the smoke-blackened parish church. Bear left on to **Lower Kirkgate**, then right on to **Bank Bottom**. Cross **Hebble Brook** and walk uphill; where the road bears sharp left, keep straight ahead up a steep cobbled lane. When you meet a road, go right for about 200yds (183m). Just after the entrance to a warehouse (Aquaspersion), take a cobbled path on the left that makes a steep ascent up **Beacon Hill**.

② This old packhorse track – known as the **Magna Via** – joins another path and continues uphill to a large retaining wall, where you have a choice of tracks. Keep left on a cinder track, slightly downhill, as views open up of the surprisingly rural **Shibden Valley**. Keep left when the track forks again; after a further 100yds (91m) take a walled path on the left (signed to **Stump Cross**). Follow a hedgerow downhill through a little estate of new houses to a road. Cross here and take a gated path immediately to the right of a farm entrance, which takes you downhill, under the railway line and into **Shibden Park**, close to the boating lake.

③ Follow a drive uphill. Near the top of the hill you will find a footpath on the left, giving access to the Elizabethan splendour of **Shibden Hall** itself. Otherwise, continue uphill; just before you meet the main A58 road, bear right, down **Old Godley Lane**. Pass houses and take steps up to the main road at the busy junction of **Stump Cross**.

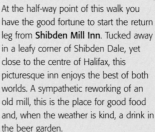

WHERE TO EAT AND DRINK
At the half-way point of this walk you have the good fortune to start the return leg from **Shibden Mill Inn**. Tucked away in a leafy corner of Shibden Dale, yet close to the centre of Halifax, this picturesque inn enjoys the best of both worlds. A sympathetic reworking of an old mill, this is the place for good food and, when the weather is kind, a drink in the beer garden.

④ Cross over the road and take **Staups Lane**, to the left of the **Stump Cross Inn**. Walk up the lane, which soon becomes cobbled, to meet another surfaced road. Bear left here, down a metalled track, through a gate, to join a straight, double-paved track into **Shibden Dale**. When the paving ends, continue via a gate and through open pasture. Turn left, at the next gate, walking down a lane that soon leads you to the **Shibden Mill Inn**.

⑤ Walk to the far end of the pub's car park, to join a track that crosses **Shibden Beck**. Beyond a brick-built house, the track narrows to a walled path. You emerge from countryside, to walk past the houses of **Claremont** and cross the main A58 road, as it goes through the steep-sided **Godley Cutting**, on a bridge. Take a set of steps immediately after the bridge and walk left along the road. From here you can retrace your route of earlier in the day, back into **Halifax**.

WHILE YOU'RE THERE
As well as the **Piece Hall**, which houses an art gallery and several craft shops, you should acquire a child and visit **Eureka!**, the ultimate in hands-on discovery museums. It is designed specifically for children up to the age of 12, with over 400 interactive exhibits exploring science, nature and the world around you.

WHAT TO LOOK FOR
The birds-eye view of Halifax from **Beacon Hill** is well worth the effort of climbing it. A century ago this view would have looked very different: most people's idea of William Blake's 'dark satanic mills' were here in unhealthy profusion, casting a dense pall of sulphurous smoke over the valley.

Gristhorpe Man and His Landscape

A walk in North Yorkshire's eastern extremity, where prehistoric man lived and died.

•DISTANCE•	5 miles (8km)
•MINIMUM TIME•	2hrs
•ASCENT / GRADIENT•	249ft (75m) ▲ ▲ ▲
•LEVEL OF DIFFICULTY•	🚶 🚶 🚶
•PATHS•	Field paths and tracks, muddy after rain, 11 stiles
•LANDSCAPE•	Hillside, then flat farmland
•SUGGESTED MAP•	aqua3 OS Explorer 301 Scarborough, Bridlington & Flamborough Head
•START / FINISH•	Grid reference: TA 096796
•DOG FRIENDLINESS•	Livestock in fields, so dogs on leads
•PARKING•	Street parking in Muston, near the Ship Inn
•PUBLIC TOILETS•	None on route

BACKGROUND TO THE WALK

A little inland from the rocky peninsula of Filey Brigg, which marks the end (or the start) of both the Cleveland Way and the Wolds Way, is peaceful pasture and arable land bounded on the south by the first slopes of the chalk escarpment of the Yorkshire Wolds. It is fertile land, once wet with bog but long-since drained and farmed. The local name for this landscape – Carr – is from an Old Norse word meaning boggy ground.

Early Inhabitants

Some of Britain's earliest inhabitants lived around here – not, like their successors, on the Wolds themselves, but in refuges among the reeds and willows. Most of the details of their civilisation have long since disappeared, with burial sites vanishing under the plough. Fortunately, however, we know much about one inhabitant, now known as Gristhorpe Man, whose remains are now on display in the Rotunda Museum in Scarborough.

Gristhorpe Man

In 1834 workmen, employed by the local landowner in Gristhorpe, dug into a tumulus near the village. Under a covering of oak branches they uncovered a coffin lid carved with a face (which they later trampled on and made unrecognisable!). The coffin was made from a single oak log, with lichened bark still adhering to it. Inside was the complete skeleton of a man, more than six feet tall, with his legs drawn up to his chest. His body had been wrapped in fine animal skin, secured by a bone pin. With him were a bronze dagger head and a bone pommel for it, as well as a flint knife. By his side was a bark dish stitched with strips of animal skin or sinew. It is believed that he is probably more than 4000 years old.

You will get a fine view of Gristhorpe Man's homeland from the first part of the walk as you ascend from Muston on to the slopes of Flotmanby Wold. This is part of the long distance Wolds Way, which runs 79½ miles (127km) from Hessle Haven on the banks of the

Humber to Filey Brigg. If the weather is decent, you will be able to see the Brigg to the north east while, further to the north, Scarborough is clearly visible.

The Carrs

The walk descends along an ancient hollow way route, and on to the watery peat landscape of The Carrs, which are criss-crossed with drainage ditches that include the evocatively-named Old Scurf and the channelled River Hertford, which was cut in 1807. You will cross the Hull-to-Scarborough railway line by the former railway station for Gristhorpe village. The walk returns by field paths and tracks across Muston Carr and through Muston Bottoms to the village, which is worth exploring for its range of excellent vernacular houses, many built of chalk, with their typical pantiled roofs.

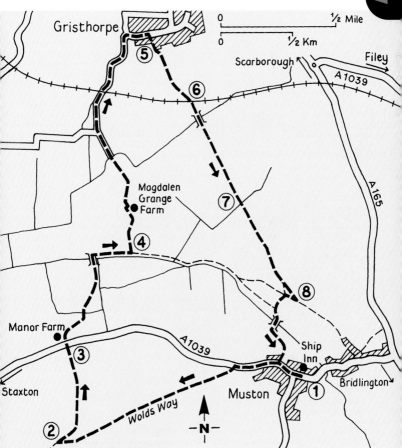

Walk 37 **Directions**

① From the **Ship Inn**, walk in the direction of **Folkton**. Just before the **Muston** village sign on the right, take a waymarked stile in the hedge

on your left, signed '**Wolds Way**'. Go forward to meet a track, and follow the **Wolds Way** signs uphill over two waymarked stiles. At the top right hand corner of the next field go over a stile and continue ahead to the next sign post.

Walk 37

② Turn right down the track, following the bridleway sign. Continue downhill, in this hollow way, then across two fields to a main road.

③ Cross the road and walk through the farm buildings, bearing right along the track. Cross the river on a concrete bridge.

④ At the end of the bridge turn right along the riverside and follow the track to the next bridge, where you turn left up the waymarked track. Follow the track along the edge of the farm buildings. It swings right at the end of them and, at a crossroads of tracks, turn left towards the red roofed houses. The track becomes metalled and goes over a level crossing. Follow the road as it bends right into the main street of **Gristhorpe**.

> **WHERE TO EAT AND DRINK**
> The walk begins and ends at the **Ship Inn** in Muston, which offers bar meals and snacks, as well as traditional Sunday lunches. Just off the route, the **Bull Inn** at the eastern end of Gristhorpe village also offers meals and snacks, and welcomes children.

⑤ Opposite **Briar Cottage** take a signed public footpath to the right and go through a metal gate, then beside some farm buildings to a stile beside another metal gate. Follow the track down the field and over another stile, then half left across the field towards a railway crossing.

⑥ Go through the white kissing gates at the crossing, then continue across the field to two stiles at either end of a footbridge. Continue ahead up the ridge to a stile in the top right-hand corner of the field.

> **WHAT TO LOOK FOR**
> The soil under your feet will tell you a great deal about the **geology** of this easternmost part of North Yorkshire. On the first part of the walk you will find the light, dryer soils that are typical of the chalk landscape of the Wolds – sometimes chalk nodules can be found on the surface. By contrast, The Carrs has rich peat soils, in places almost black. When I was last here Magdalen Grange Farm was almost surrounded by an inky landscape, where the fields had been newly-ploughed.

After another small field go across a plank bridge and over a stile. Continue ahead with the fence on your right. On reaching the telegraph pole, go through an opening in the hedge and continue with the fence now on your left-hand side. Go over a stile and continue straight ahead. The path becomes a grassy track. Go through a metal gate on to another track, continuing to meet a crossing track.

⑦ Turn right, following the bridleway sign. Go over a stile beside a metal gate then follow the hedge on your left as it bends left. Follow the path along the field edge, go through a gateway, then across a bridge, through another gateway and bend left on to the track, which you follow to a kissing gate on to the main road. Turn left back to the village centre.

> **WHAT TO LOOK FOR**
> Visit **Filey Brigg**, the rocky promontory that punctuates the coast between Flamborough Head and the castle-crowned headland at Scarborough. You can explore the rock pools for shellfish and small marine creatures, and reflect on visits by Charlotte Brontë and by RD Blackmore, who set part of his novel *Mary Anerley* here.

Kendal's Two Castles

Visit two ancient castles, on opposite banks of the River Kent.

•DISTANCE•	3 miles (4.8km)
•MINIMUM TIME•	1hr 30min
•ASCENT / GRADIENT•	300ft (91m) ▲▲▲
•LEVEL OF DIFFICULTY•	🚶🚶 🚶🚶 🚶🚶
•PATHS•	Pavements, surfaced and grassy paths with steps, no stiles
•LANDSCAPE•	Historic Kendal and open hillside
•SUGGESTED MAP•	aqua3 OS Explorer OL 7 The English Lakes (SE)
•START / FINISH•	Grid reference: SD 518928
•DOG FRIENDLINESS•	Open hillside grazed by sheep, busy roads through town
•PARKING•	Free parking area by river (occasionally occupied by fairground), numerous pay car parks near by
•PUBLIC TOILETS•	Near road bridge, Miller Bridge, end of river parking area

BACKGROUND TO THE WALK

Known as the 'Auld Grey Town', because of the colour of its predominantly limestone buildings, enterprising Kendal retains much of its original character. Until recently Kendal was the administrative centre for the former county of Westmorland. Sited either side of the River Kent its occupation stretches from Roman times to the present day and its varied stone buildings, nooks, crannies, yards and castles offer a rich historical tapestry. This walk visits two important strongholds located strategically on high ground either side of the river; Kendal Castle and Castle Howe.

Kendal Castle

Sited in a commanding position over Kendal and the River Kent, the ruined Kendal Castle is quietly impressive and offers fine views in all directions. The people of Kendal know it as an old friend and may tell you that here was the birthplace of Catherine Parr who became Henry VIII's sixth and last wife in 1543. Although her grandfather, William Parr who died in 1483, lies entombed in Kendal parish church, apparently there is no evidence that Catherine ever set foot in Kendal and the castle was probably falling into decay by that time.

It is thought that Kendal Castle succeeded Castle Howe, sited opposite on the western side of the river, sometime in the late 12th century. After the Norman barons had secured the kingdom they required suitable quarters with sufficient space to administer their feudal territories and so replaced their chiefly wooden motte and bailey castles with castles of stone. Initial timber buildings surrounded by a ditch and small tower were replaced by new stone buildings in about 1220 and work continued until 1280 by one of the early barons of Kendal, either Gilbert Fitzrheinfred or his son William de Lancaster.

Today, the ruins of Kendal Castle consist of a circular defensive wall and three towers plus a residential gatehouse surrounded by a partly filled ditch. The entrance path leads through the wall at the point where a gatehouse once stood. To the left are the largest standing remains, the house where the baron's family lived, known as the Lyons Den, or Machell Tower. To the right, a favourite climb for adventurous children, stands the Troutbeck Tower sporting its 'dungeon room' below and garderobe (toilet), with free fall into the

Walk 38

ditch/moat, above. If you do climb the tower, and it may be against regulations to do so, don't fall through the unprotected hole. It could be both extremely dangerous and highly embarrassing. South of the compound is a lesser tower and the exit here, a former gatehouse, is now barred by a locked door.

The Parr family occupied the castle for four generations, from 1380 to 1486, when William Parr's widow remarried and move to Northamptonshire. The demise of the castle took place at a pace after this and much of the stone is thought to have been recycled for use in building works in the 'Auld Grey Town' below.

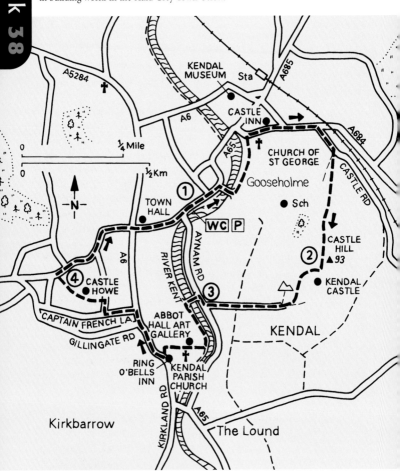

Walk 38 Directions

① Walk upstream along the riverside parking area to a footbridge crossing the river. Cross and bear left to follow the surfaced walkway, through Gooseholme. At the junction of roads by the **Church** of St George turn right down **Castle Street**. Pass the **Castle Inn** and join **Ann Street**. Turn right and continue up the hill to **Castle Road** on the right. Ascend Castle Road to where a kissing gate on the right leads on to Castle Hill. Follow the broad path ascending the shoulder to the ruins of **Kendal Castle**.

② Round the castle ruins until, at a point beneath its southern end, a path can be found dropping down to the right. Descend steeply to pass through an iron kissing gate on to **Sunnyside Road**. Follow Sunnyside, which becomes **Parr Street**, and exit on to **Aynam Road**.

> **WHAT TO LOOK FOR** ⓘ
>
> **Castle Howe**, Kendal's first Norman motte and bailey castle, was built between 1068 and 1100. At the time it was the cutting northern edge of the rapidly established Norman kingdom and Kendal, then known as Kirkbie Strickland, was mentioned in the Domesday survey of 1086. The obelisk on top of Castle Howe was designed by Francis Webster and built by William Holme in 1778. It was dedicated to the 'Glorious Revolution' of 1688 when William of Orange replaced James II. It is known locally as 'Bill Holmes' bodkin'.

③ Turn right along Aynam Road to a crossing. Cross and find a footbridge leading over the **River Kent**. Over the river bear left, downstream, and walk a short distance to a narrow, surfaced path leading right. Continue along the path, lined by yew trees and limestone coping stones, to pass between **Kendal parish church** and **Abbot Hall Art Gallery**. Emerge on to the **Kirkland Road**, the main road through Kendal, by the impressive iron gates of the church with the **Ring O'Bells** pub to the left. Turn right along the road and proceed 300yds (274m) to a

> **WHERE TO EAT AND DRINK** ⓘ
>
> Kendal is famed for its many fine pubs and there is a plethora of cafés and restaurants. On this walk you pass the **Castle Inn** and the **Ring O'Bells**. Both offer real ale and bar meals. In Kirkland there are several fish and chip shops and take-aways. The **Brewery Arts Centre**, just beyond Captain French Lane along Highgate, has both café and bar facilities.

crossing. Cross it then bear right to cross **Gillingate Road** and keep along the main road, now called **Highgate**. At Lightfoot's chemist shop go left up **Captain French Lane** for 300yds (274m) then go right up **Garth Heads Lane**. Follow this until a steep path ascends to the left. Steps lead to a terrace and a view out over Kendal. Cross the grass terrace towards the mound and its distinct bodkin-shaped obelisk. Climb the steps then spiral left until, as the path levels, steps lead up right to the obelisk and the top of **Castle Howe**.

④ Return to the path and go right. Find a gap on the left and emerge on the road at the top of **Beast Banks**. Descend the hill, which becomes **Allhallows Lane**, to the traffic lights and pedestrian crossing opposite the **Town Hall**. Cross the road and go left and then immediately right down **Lowther Street**. Go left at the bottom to a zebra crossing beyond the **Holy Trinity of St George,** which leads to the riverside.

> **WHILE YOU'RE THERE** ⓘ
>
> **Kendal Museum**, **Abbot Hall Art Gallery** and **Kendal parish church** are all centres of attraction. The former, with everything from stuffed bears and crocodiles to neolithic Langdale stone axes has long held a fascination for me. There are so many interesting buildings and features in Kendal, the history so rich and varied, it is impossible to single out individual items. Have a roam and afterwards know that there are numerous quiet places on the banks of the River Kent, reputedly England's fastest flowing river and once a huge source of power for this the 'Auld Grey Town', to eat your fish and chips.

Walk 39

Cat Bells and High Spy

A delightful romp high above two lovely valleys steeped in industrial history.

•DISTANCE•	9 miles (14.5km)
•MINIMUM TIME•	4hrs
•ASCENT / GRADIENT•	2,460ft (750m) ▲▲▲
•LEVEL OF DIFFICULTY•	🚶 🚶 🚶 (Not advised in poor visibility)
•PATHS•	Generally good paths, indistinct above Tongue Gill, 4 stiles
•LANDSCAPE•	Fell ridge tops, quarry workings, woodland, riverside path
•SUGGESTED MAP•	aqua3 OS Explorer OL 4 The English Lakes (NW)
•START / FINISH•	Grid reference: NY 247212
•DOG FRIENDLINESS•	No special problems, though fell sheep roam tops
•PARKING•	Wooded parking area at Hawes End
•PUBLIC TOILETS•	None on route

BACKGROUND TO THE WALK

Both Borrowdale and the Newlands Valley, like many parts of Lakeland, have seen extensive periods of industry from an early age. From the top of Maiden Moor scree can be seen issuing from the workings of an old mine in Newlands. This is Goldscope, a name that first appears in records during the reign of Elizabeth I, who imported German miners to work here. The name is a corruption of 'Gottesgab' or 'God's gift', so called because it was one of the most prosperous mines in Lakeland.

Copper was mined here as early as the 13th century from a vein 9ft (2.7m) thick. The mine also produced large quantities of lead, a small amount of silver and a modicum of gold. The mine's greatest period of production was in the 16th century, when Elizabeth made a serious attempt to exploit England's own resources to reduce dependency on imports. Ironically, it was German miners who largely worked Goldscope, encouraged by the award of hidden subsidies in the form of waived taxes. Copper ore was taken by packhorse to the shores of Derwent Water by way of Little Town. It was then transported to a smelter on the banks of the River Greta, at Brigham. From here the copper went to the Receiving House, now the Moot Hall, in Keswick, to receive the Queen's Mark.

The Rigghead Quarries in Tongue Gill produced slate from levels cut deep into the fellside and a number of adits are still open, though they are dangerous and should not be explored. But the real secret of these fells is wad, more commonly known as graphite, plumbago or black cawke – or the lead in your pencil. Its discovery dates from the early 16th century when trees uprooted in a storm revealed a black mineral on their roots. Shepherds soon realised that the substance was useful for marking sheep, and later for making metal castings and as a lubricant. Its other uses included a fixing agent for blue dyes, glazing pottery, a rust preventative, polishing iron and for casting shells and cannon balls.

Pencils, for which graphite was ultimately destined, didn't appear until around 1660, and then as wooden sticks with a piece of graphite fitted into the tip. As a result, Keswick became the world centre of the graphite and pencil industries. The first record of a factory making pencils appears in 1832. The Cumberland Pencil Company was first set up in nearby Braithwaite in 1868 and moved to its present site in Keswick 30 years later.

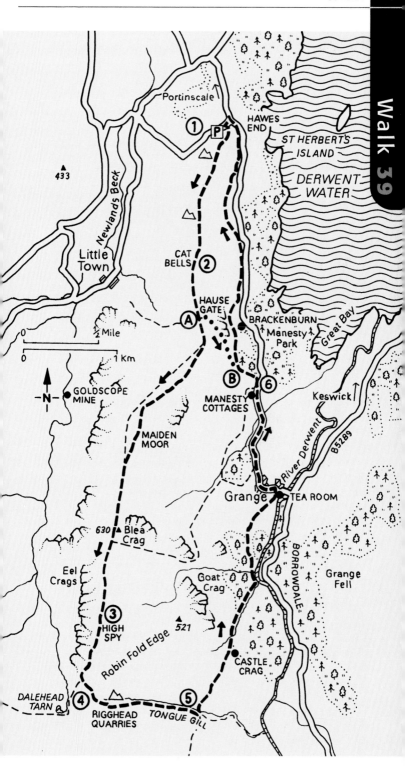

Walk 39 Directions

① At **Hawes End**, walk up the road and at a bend take a stepped and rocky path rising steeply. Follow this, climbing steadily through small rocky outcrops before reaching **Brandlehow**. The onward route keeps to the centre of a grassy ridge, before rising through more rock outcrops to **Cat Bells**.

② From Cat Bells descend easily to the broad col of **Hause Gate**. This is Point Ⓐ. Go forward across Hause Gate on a grassy path and on to the broad expanse of **Maiden Moor**, across which a good path leads to the summit of **High Spy**.

③ Head down a path towards the col housing **Dalehead Tarn**. Gradually, the ravine of **Tongue Gill** appears over to the left, but finding the right moment to quit the Dalehead Tarn path is a hit and miss affair. Such paths as there are across to Tongue Gill are indistinct and invariably wet underfoot, but just keep heading for a fence.

④ Either of the stiles across the fence gives on to a path leading to a large cairn at the start of a path down to **Rigghead Quarries**. Take care descending the steep slate paths until the gradient eases alongside Tongue Gill itself. Keeping to the right bank, follow the gill to a path T-junction, and there turn left to a gate and stile, and footbridge.

⑤ The path now climbs gently and soon crosses a shallow col near **Castle Crag**. Go past the crag, descending, shortly to enter woodland at a gate. Cross a narrow footbridge spanning **Broadslack Gill** and follow a path down to the banks of the **River Derwent**. Just before the river, cross a footbridge on the left, and another a little further on, keeping to a path roughly parallel with the river until you reach a wall. Take a broad track following the wall and eventually walk out to a surfaced lane. Go right and walk up to **Grange** village. Go left and follow the road.

⑥ Just after **Manesty Cottages**, branch left on to a path climbing gently above the road to a stile and gate. Through this, go forward on to a gently rising broad track and, when it forks, bear right, heading for a path above an intake wall. This is Point Ⓑ. Pressing on beyond **Brackenburn**, the footpath, which affords lovely views of Derwent Water, soon dips to make a brief acquaintance with the road at a small quarry car park. Beyond this gap, immediately return to a gently rising path, this is an old road, traversing the lower slopes of Cat Bells that will ultimately bring you back to the road at **Hawes End**.

WHILE YOU'RE THERE

Consider taking in **Castle Crag**. The ascent and descent from the main path is clear enough, but it is steep and not suitable for very young children. But what a fabulous viewpoint! To the east, the white-cottaged village of Rosthwaite sits comfortably against a backdrop of hummocky fells and steep crags, while looking northwards you'll see one of the finest views of Derwent Water, the Vale of Keswick and Skiddaw beyond.

WHERE TO EAT AND DRINK

Grange Bridge Cottage Tea Room in the village of Grange offers a range of teas and snacks throughout the year (reduced opening hours in winter).

Romans and Countryfolk of Corbridge

Discover little Corbridge, where history lies around every corner.

•DISTANCE•	6 miles (9.7km)
•MINIMUM TIME•	3hrs 30min
•ASCENT / GRADIENT•	525ft (160m) ▲▲▲
•LEVEL OF DIFFICULTY•	🚶 🚶 🚶
•PATHS•	Village streets, riverside and farm paths and lanes, 8 stiles
•LANDSCAPE•	Small town and low hills
•SUGGESTED MAP•	aqua3 OS Explorer OL43 Hadrian's Wall
•START / FINISH•	Grid reference: NY 992642
•DOG FRIENDLINESS•	Dogs should be on leads
•PARKING•	On town centre streets
•PUBLIC TOILETS•	On Princess Street between Hill Street and Main Street

BACKGROUND TO THE WALK

Corbridge is a picturesque little town, with Georgian stone cottages, antique shops and old inns cuddled up to a square-towered church. Nothing much happens here these days: people come for a little peace and quiet away from the city and maybe a spot of Sunday lunch in one of those inns. The wide River Tyne flows by lazily on a journey that takes it from the wild hills of Northumberland, through the cityscapes of Newcastle and onwards to the shivering North Sea.

Roman Settlement

Though the present town was founded in Saxon times, the Romans, under Agricola, first arrived in AD 79. They established their settlement six years later, just ½ mile (800m) to the west of modern Corbridge, on the north bank of the Tyne. Known as Corstopitum, it would have been the most northerly settlement in the Roman Empire, strategically placed at the junction of their Dere Street (York to northern Britain) and Stanegate (Corbridge to Carlisle) roads, and near to what was, after AD 122, the frontier, Hadrian's Wall. The Romans also had a fine bridge across the Tyne, and you can still see the rubble remains of foundations when the water levels are low.

Defence against the Scots

In past centuries Corbridge was second only to Newcastle in this part of the world, and of great strategic importance. As such, the town has known many troubled times. You'll see that straight away, for the first house you come to, Low Hall on Main Street, has a fortified pele tower. These fortifications were added to defend against the Scots; both the marauding Border reivers, who came to rob and pillage, and the Scots armies, who came to destroy. William Wallace, Robert the Bruce and King David II all invaded and all laid the town waste on their journeys south. Centrepiece of modern Corbridge is undoubtedly St Andrews Church, built in the Saxon era and with a Roman archway borrowed from the older settlement. The church was extensively modified in the 13th century, with the addition of

Walk 40

aisles, transepts and chancel, and was restored during Victorian times.

Round the back of the church you'll come across another fortified house, this time the 13th-century Vicar's Pele – even the clergy were not immune to the wrath of the Scots. Before going down to the River Tyne and that magnificent 17th-century bridge, the route passes Town Barns, where the famous north-east based author Catherine Cookson lived in the 1970s.

We take a short riverside ramble now, before climbing out of the valley, traversing pastures scattered with woods, and strolling along hedge-lined country lanes. You arrive at Prospect Hill, with its pristine cottages and farmhouses. It does indeed have prospects – a fine view of Corbridge, the Tyne Valley and the low hills beyond where the Romans marched and Hadrian's Wall once offered a firm deterrent to those erring northerners.

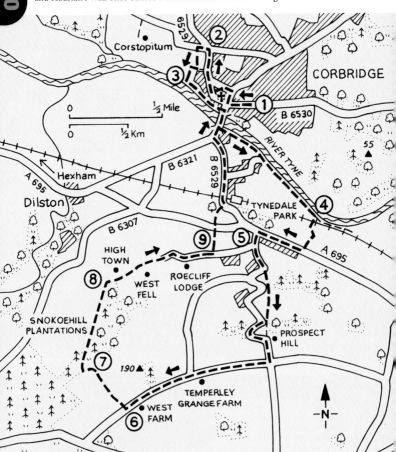

Walk 40 Directions

① The walk begins at **Low Hall Pele** on the eastern end of **Main Street**. Head west down Main Street before turning right up **Princes Street**. At the town hall turn left along **Hill Street**, then, just before the church, turn left up the narrow street to pass the **Vicar's Pele**. Turn right at the **Market Place** and head north up **Watling Street**, then **Stagshaw Road**, which is

Walk 40

> **WHILE YOU'RE THERE**
> Visit the Roman Fort, **Corstopitum**, where the two large granaries and the Fountain House are particularly impressive. The main street that runs through is the Stanegate. Finds from the archaeological digs are kept in the museum. They include Roman armour, coins and other personal artefacts.

staggered to the left beyond the **Wheatsheaf Inn**.

② Go left along **Trinity Terrace** then left again along a footpath, signed 'West Green'. This leads past Catherine Cookson's old house, **Town Barns**, to the Georgian house of **Orchard Vale**, where you turn right, then left along a lane to the river.

③ Turn left along **Carelgate**, then follow the riverside path to the town bridge. Go over the bridge, then follow the south banks of the Tyne on an unsurfaced track that passes the cricket ground at **Tynedale Park** before mounting a grassy embankment running parallel to the river.

④ Turn right up some steps, go over a ladder stile, then cross the railway tracks (with care). Another stile and some more steps lead the path through a wood and across a field to meet the **A695** where you turn right – there's a footpath on the nearside.

⑤ Just beyond some cottages, turn left up a country lane, which zig-zags up **Prospect Hill**. Just after the first bend leave the lane for a southbound path that climbs fields. Just short of some woods the path meets a track where you turn right for a few paces to rejoin the lane.

Follow this up to reach a crossroads at the top of the hill, where you turn right.

⑥ After passing **Temperley Grange** and **West farms** leave the road for a path on the right that follows first the right-hand side, then the left-hand side of a dry-stone wall across high fields and down to the **Snokoehill Plantations**.

> **WHERE TO EAT AND DRINK**
> The **Angel** on Main Street is a large 17th-century coaching inn that offers a fine range of tasty meals, including Sunday roasts. It's a free house with Black Sheep and Courage ales always available. Children are welcome.

⑦ Go through a gate to enter the wood, then turn left along a track running along the top edge. The track doubles back to the right, soon to follow the bottom edge of the woods.

⑧ Turn right beyond a gate above **High Town farm** and follow the track, which becomes tarred beyond **West Fell**.

⑨ Beyond **Roecliff Lodge** a path on the left crosses a field to reach the **A695** road. Across the other side of the road the path continues and enters a copse known as **The Scrogs**, before joining the **B6529** by **Corbridge Railway Station**. Follow this over the bridge and back into **Corbridge** itself.

> **WHAT TO LOOK FOR**
> In an old stableyard wall behind the Wheatsheaf Inn (off Watling Street) there are two crudely **sculpted heads** believed to have come from one of the three Corbridge churches set ablaze by the invading Scots in the early 14th century.

Smugglers and the Light of Marsden Bay

Along the coast near South Shields, and inland to the Cleadon Hills.

•DISTANCE•	5½ miles (9km)
•MINIMUM TIME•	2hrs
•ASCENT / GRADIENT•	246ft (75m) ▲ ▲ ▲
•LEVEL OF DIFFICULTY•	🚶🚶 🚶🚶 🚶🚶
•PATHS•	Roads, tracks, field and coastal paths
•LANDSCAPE•	Views to sea, with offshore rocks, rolling countryside
•SUGGESTED MAP•	aqua3 OS Explorer 316 Newcastle upon Tyne
•START / FINISH•	Grid reference: NZ 412635
•DOG FRIENDLINESS•	On leads on inland section of walk
•PARKING•	Whitburn Coastal Park car park, signed off A183 – turn right after entrance and drive to southern end of road
•PUBLIC TOILETS•	None on route

BACKGROUND TO THE WALK

The coast of Durham south of the Tyne was long renowned for its smugglers. The natural caves at the base of the cliffs of Marsden Bay provided hiding places for illicit activity. Most famous of the smugglers was Jack the Blaster, who in 1792 used explosives to increase the size of one of the caves, and provide steps from the cliff top. An entrepreneur, he sold refreshments to other smugglers. In the 19th century an underground ballroom was created here, and in the 1930s a lift was installed. It is now a popular pub and eating place called the Marsden Grotto.

The Punishment Hanging

One 18th-century smuggler turned informer to the customs men. His fellows discovered his treachery, and the smugglers' ship was prevented from landing its contraband cargo. As punishment the man was hanged in a basket in a shaft, now called Smugglers' Hole, near the Grotto, where he starved to death. On stormy nights his shrieks are said to be heard in the howling of the wind.

The Windmills of Cleadon

On the walk you will pass two windmills. The first, in Marsden, is a squat building that still retains its sails. The other, higher on Cleadon Hills, was built in the 1820s, and survived until the end of the century, when it was damaged in a storm. In World War Two it housed Royal Observer Corps members who scanned the North Sea for enemy aeroplanes. Looking south from the tower you will see the Greek temple that is the Penshaw Monument. A half-sized replica of the Temple of Theseus in Athens, it commemorates the 1st Earl of Durham, 'Radical Jack' Lambton, first Governor of Canada. As you cross the golf course beyond the windmill there are views north to Tynemouth, with its castle and priory on the headland north of the river.

The red-and-white striped Souter Lighthouse was opened in 1871 to protect ships from the notorious rocks called Whitburn Steel, just off the coast. It was the first light in the world to be electrically powered, by electric alternators. Originally it was nearly ¼ mile (400m) from the sea, but erosion has brought the cliff edge much nearer. Now decommissioned and in the care of the National Trust, the lighthouse and its surrounding buildings reward careful exploration. The grassy area north of the light, The Lees, was farmed until the 1930s, and then given to the local council as a park. The industrial buildings by the road are the remains of lime kilns, used by the local limestone quarries. South of the light, where Whitburn Coastal Park now lies, was from 1873 to 1968 the site of Whitburn Colliery.

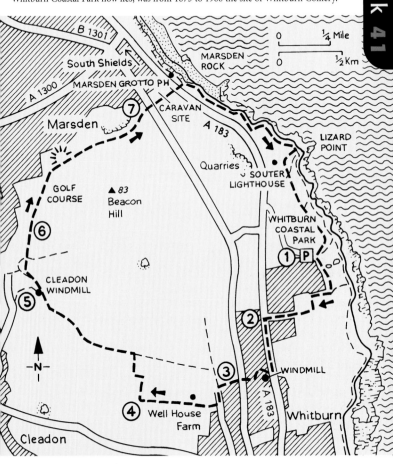

Walk 41 Directions

① Leave the car park at its southern end, following the gravel track toward the houses. The path winds and goes past a sign for **Whitburn Point Nature Reserve**. Follow the track ahead to go through a gap in a wall and turn

right. The path bends right, left and right again to join a road into houses. Go straight ahead to join the main road.

② Cross the road and turn left. Walk down the road until you reach the **windmill**. Turn right to enter the grounds of the windmill. Go up the slope on the path and then between houses. Bear left then turn right to reach a T-junction.

③ Go straight ahead on a path that goes to the right of house **No 99**. When you reach another road turn left. Just after the first bungalow on the right, turn right along a signed track. Follow the track towards the farm. Go through the farmyard over two stiles and follow the lane beyond, with a hedge to your right. Where it ends, turn right over a stile.

WHILE YOU'RE THERE ⓘ

Visit **Arbeia Roman Fort** in South Shields. Built to supply the Roman army's campaign against the northern tribes, it has a full-size reconstruction of its gateway and a museum where you can see how Roman soldiers lived. You may even meet a member of the 'Cohors Quinta Gallorum' – volunteers dressed in Roman uniform.

---

④ Follow the path along the field edge. Go over another stile, gradually ascending. The path bends left then right, still following the field edge. Go over another two stiles. The path will bring you to the tower of **Cleadon Windmill**.

⑤ Go to the right of the windmill, following the wall on your right. Go right through a kissing gate, then bear slightly right (a brick tower to your left). Go parallel with the wall

---

WHERE TO EAT AND DRINK ⓘ

The **Marsden Grotto** near Marsden Rock has a restaurant, bar and bistro, catering for all tastes, from snacks to full meals (children welcome until 8:30PM, no dogs except guide dogs). Further south, **Souter Lighthouse** (children and guide dogs welcome) has a good National Trust tea room, with the chance to sit in the walled garden on sunny days – when the foghorn won't be working!

---

on your right. Cross a track and go through a wire mesh fence at right angles to the wall. Follow the path through scrubland to emerge by a yellow post by the **golf course**.

⑥ Cross the course, following the yellow posts and looking out for golfers. Go over a stone stile and turn right along a signed footpath, following the wall on your right. The path eventually descends beside houses to a road.

⑦ Cross and take the footpath almost opposite, to the right of a caravan site, heading towards the sea. Carefully cross the busy **A183** then turn right, following the sea edge. **Marsden Rock** is near by, and the **Marsden Grotto** to your left as you cross the road. Follow the coast as it bends left to **Lizard Point**. After a visit to **Souter Lighthouse**, continue ahead on a path slightly inland from the coast, which returns you to the car park.

WHAT TO LOOK FOR ⓘ

Off the coast at Marsden Bay are numerous **sea stacks** – pillars of rock that have been left as the sea has eroded the cliffs. The most famous of them is the largest, known as Marsden Rock. Although still impressive, it barely does justice to its fame. Until 1996 the rock was a naturally-formed arch; a second, smaller stack was joined to the rock on its south east side with a bridge of limestone. When this collapsed, the smaller stack had to be demolished as it was in a dangerous state. In the past there were ladders that gave access to the top for those willing to wade out, and local people used to have picnics there. There are even reports of choirs and brass bands giving impromptu concerts.

Criffel and New Abbey

A 13th-century love story of the Lady Devorgilla, set forever in stone.

•DISTANCE•	3¾ miles (6km)
•MINIMUM TIME•	3hrs
•ASCENT / GRADIENT•	1,686ft (514m) ▲▲▲
•LEVEL OF DIFFICULTY•	🏃 🏃 🏃
•PATHS•	Forest road, rough hill and wood tracks, 1 stile
•LANDSCAPE•	Hills, tidal estuary, woods and pasture
•SUGGESTED MAP•	aqua3 OS Explorer 313 Dumfries & Dalbeattie
•START / FINISH•	Grid reference: NX 971634
•DOG FRIENDLINESS•	Keep on lead near livestock
•PARKING•	Car park at Ardwall farm
•PUBLIC TOILETS•	None on route

BACKGROUND TO THE WALK

The majestic ruins of Sweetheart Abbey dominate the village of New Abbey. Set against the backdrop of Criffel, Dumfries's highest hill, they stand as testimony to one woman's love, devotion and determination.

A Lasting Memorial

Sweetheart Abbey was founded in 1273 by Devorgilla, Lady of Galloway, as a memorial to her late husband, John Balliol, and as a last resting place for them both. When Balliol died at Barnard Castle in 1269, Devorgilla had his heart removed from his corpse, embalmed and placed in a silver mounted ivory casket which she carried everywhere with her.

Devorgilla lived long enough to see the graceful abbey rise beside the River Nith. She died in 1289 at Barnard Castle, Durham, and her body was carried to Dumfries, her last journey following that of her husband through the north of England into Scotland. She was interred at Sweetheart Abbey, next to her husband near the high altar, and the cask containing his heart was placed on her breast. Her devotion and attachment to her husband led the monks to give the abbey the name *dulce cor* or sweet heart. Within the abbey there can still be seen a, now headless, effigy of her holding the casket.

Originally the abbey was called New Abbey, to distinguish it from the nearby mother house of Dundrennan, and so the village that subsequently grew up around it took its name. At the Reformation, supported by the local population and the powerful Maxwell family, the abbot, Gilbert Brown, refused to give up the abbey. Eventually, in 1610, after two evictions and arrests, he was finally sent into exile.

The villagers had considerable affection for the abbey and, in 1779, started a fund to ensure its preservation. Now under the care of Historic Scotland, it remains one of the most impressive abbey ruins in Scotland. Although the roof has gone, the cruciform church and massive central tower, built from red Dumfriesshire sandstone, still stand.

The monks of Dundrennan, Glenluce and New Abbey were members of the Order of the Cistercians founded in 1098 at Cîteaux in Burgundy. Directed by the rule of St Benedict they observed a life of poverty, chastity and obedience. In 1136, some white monks of this order travelled north from Rievaulx, in Yorkshire, to found the abbey at Melrose and six years later came to Dundrennan. At the time of Devorgilla's death, there were 11 Cistercian monasteries in Scotland.

Although they lived an austere life the Cistercians played an important part in the trading network. They were the largest producers of wool in the country, at their peak accounting for around 5 per cent of Scotland's total wool production. They provided much needed employment and helped establish towns and burghs throughout the country.

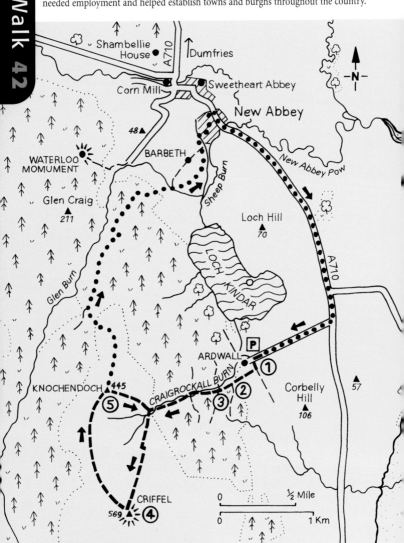

Walk 42 Directions

① From the car park head towards **Ardwall farm** then go through a gate on the left. Turn right after

70yds (64m) then head towards the hill on a track between dry-stone walls. When the road curves left, in front of the wood, take the rough track off to the right. (The Criffel Walk sign has fallen from its post.)

Walk 42

② Follow a well-trodden track uphill and through the trees following the course of the **Craigrockall Burn**. The path narrows in places and the ground is very uneven with several large boulders to climb over or around. Many trees have been felled here and it is not long before you emerge from the woods on to open hillside.

③ When you reach a T-junction with a forest road, keep straight ahead to pick up the trail on the other side and continue uphill. The ground can be very boggy, even in summer, and care needs to be taken. Cross another forest road and eventually reach a fence marking where the tree line used to be. Cross the stile here and veer to the left, heading towards the summit of **Criffel**.

WHILE YOU'RE THERE ⓘ
There's an opportunity to see how oatmeal and flour were produced at **New Abbey Corn Mill**. This classic example of a Galloway country mill is the last survivor of a once common-place industry. The fully restored, working, 18th-century mill is powered by a waterwheel and offers regular demonstrations of the miller's trade.

④ From the OS triangulation pillar on the summit of Criffel you will have a view into four kingdoms. Across the Solway to the south is England and the hills of the Lake District. A little to the right of that is the ancient Celtic kingdom of the Isle of Man, while the coast of Ireland is visible to the west. The ancient Scotti tribe came from Ireland and founded the kingdom of Scotland. On a good day the summit of Criffel is the best restaurant in town, provided you have remembered to pack the food.

WHERE TO EAT AND DRINK ⓘ
Conveniently situated right at the entrance to Sweetheart Abbey is the **Abbey Cottage tea room** where visitors can enjoy anything from a cup of tea and a scone to snacks and light meals. Elsewhere in New Abbey its worth taking the time to check out the 19th-century, Tudor-style **Criffel Inn** with its superb selection of cask beers and over 120 malt whiskies. The atmospheric bar is also the best place to sample their excellent meals, freshly prepared using local produce.

When you've eaten your picnic and enjoyed the view (see What To Look For) head roughly north west from the cairn, then go north crossing over rough ground towards the broad ridge that runs from Criffel to the neighbouring hill of Knochendoch. When you intersect a narrow footpath turn right, head downhill on it then continue, ascending again now, to reach the summit of **Knochendoch**.

⑤ From the summit cairn head east and go downhill. In the summer, when the heather is particularly thick, the going can be fairly tough and you'll have to proceed slowly and with caution. Make for the fence that runs across the hill in front of you. Turn right here and follow it back to the stile. Cross the stile and retrace your steps to the bottom of the hill.

WHAT TO LOOK FOR ⓘ
From the summit of Criffel look east towards Caerlaverock Castle on the opposite bank of the River Nith. Beyond that you will be able to see the massive cooling towers of **Chapelcross** nuclear power station standing out like a sore thumb enclosed in a patchwork of lush rolling pastures, marked out by ancient dry-stone walls.

The Wells of the Rees

Take this strenuous walk along the Southern Upland Way in search of the past.

•DISTANCE•	6¼ miles (10km)
•MINIMUM TIME•	3hrs 30min
•ASCENT / GRADIENT•	558ft (170m) ▲▲▲
•LEVEL OF DIFFICULTY•	犬犬 犬犬 犬犬
•PATHS•	Forest roads, forest track, very rough ground
•LANDSCAPE•	Hills, forest and loch
•SUGGESTED MAP•	aqua3 OS Explorer 310 Glenluce & Kirkcowan
•START / FINISH•	Grid reference: NX 260735
•DOG FRIENDLINESS•	OK but keep on lead near livestock
•PARKING•	Near Derry farm
•PUBLIC TOILETS•	None on route

BACKGROUND TO THE WALK

Sitting 'on the hillside at the back of the sheiling called Kilgallioch' wrote Davie Bell, 'are three dome-shaped structures of great antiquity.' These were the Wells o' the Rees, the rees in question being sheep pens surrounding the wells.

A Determined Effort

Davie Bell, popularly known as The Highwayman, rode his bicycle all over the roughest parts of south west Scotland in the 1930s and 40s and chronicled his exploits in a weekly column in the *Ayrshire Post*. He was intrigued by the Wells o' the Rees and mounted several expeditions in search of them. Although he came close, time and again he was defeated by thick bracken and an almost featureless landscape. Today, the waymarked Southern Upland Way (SUW) takes walkers to within 100yds (91m) of the wells and a signpost points them out. But when Davie Bell was roaming these moors, often on his bicycle, but sometimes on foot, there were no long distance footpaths or signposts. Many paths and tracks would have criss-crossed the moor but they were the tracks used by herdsmen and farmers to their remote steadings.

Davie eventually found the wells after getting directions from the farmer's wife at Kilgallioch. He described them as 'three piles of stones… skilfully constructed, with each well having a canopy and the shape of the whole like that of a beehive.' Made of flat stones and oval in shape they were 'streamlined into the hillside, with a recess over the well for a utensil.' Sixty years later the people are gone but the wells remain.

This part of Galloway was sparsely populated before the forestry came, but when trees replaced sheep, shepherds and their families abandoned their lonely sheilings to ruin and decay amidst the trees. With the opening of the SUW, walkers trudge this wild landscape once again. These latter day pilgrims, follow in the footsteps of early Christians on their way to Whithorn. Although locals told Davie Bell that the wells had been built by the Romans, it seems more likely that they were made for the pilgrims. According to the Revd C H Dick in his *Highways and Byways of Galloway and Carrick*, the wells may have been part of the ancient church and graveyard of Kilgallioch, which was sited near by, although he walked across the moors from New Luce in 1916 and saw nothing in the way of ruins. The pilgrims' route to Whithorn was also the path followed by lepers on their way from Glenluce Abbey to the leper colony 1½ miles (2.4km) north of Loch Derry at Libberland. They washed in the Purgatory Burn near Laggangarn and no doubt they also stopped for refreshment at the Wells o' the Rees.

Walk 43 Directions

① Cross a cattle grid and head west along the SUW on a well-surfaced forest road. Pass **Loch Derry**, on your right in just under a mile

(1.6km), then continue on the forest road, passing a signpost on the left to **Linn's Tomb**.

② Follow the road as it curves to the right and then, following the SUW markerpost, turn left, leave

Walk 43

the road and head uphill. It's a rather steep climb from here, on a fairly well-trodden path with plenty of waymarkers.

③ Cross a forest road and continue on the uphill path heading towards the summit of **Craig Airie Fell**. Reach the summit at an Ordnance Survey trig point.

④ From the OS **triangulation pillar**, continue on a well-marked path towards a waymarker on the horizon. Turn left at the waymarker and head downhill on a footpath that twists and turns to another waymarker near the bottom. Turn right here on to another obvious trail and keep going to reach the edge of the forest.

⑤ The SUW now follows a forest ride. A short distance along here you will come to a clearing with a cairn on your left-hand side. Keep

straight ahead following the direction arrows on the waymarkers to the next clearing where a sign points left to the **Wells of the Rees**. Turn left and head downhill, through bracken, across a ruined dry-stone wall, through more bracken and then a gap in another wall. In wintertime you will find the wells easily but in summer, when the bracken is thick, you'll have to poke about a bit. The first two wells are on your right as you come through the gap and the other is off to the left.

⑥ Retrace your steps from here to the signpost and turn right. Retrace your steps to the edge of the forest and turn right, following the edge of the forest and a burn, slightly downhill to a fence. Cross this and head roughly west across rough and boggy ground towards **Craigmoddie Fell**.

⑦ Climb to the highest point then look to your left to Loch Derry then, to the right of it, Derry farm. Head in a straight line for **Derry farm** then drop down off the fell and pick up a path heading towards **Loch Derry**.

⑧ Follow this to a small patch of trees, through a gate and on to the forest road. Turn right and return to **Derry farm** and the start of the walk.

Remembering the Reivers at Newcastleton

A quiet walk through borderlands where cattle raiding was once a part of everyday life for the local inhabitants.

•DISTANCE•	5 miles (8km)
•MINIMUM TIME•	2hrs
•ASCENT / GRADIENT•	689ft (210m) ▲▲▲
•LEVEL OF DIFFICULTY•	👣 👣 👣
•PATHS•	Quiet byroads and farm tracks, one rough climb
•LANDSCAPE•	Rolling borderlands and moors
•SUGGESTED MAP•	aqua3 OS Explorer 324 Liddesdale & Kershope Forest
•START / FINISH•	Grid reference: NY 483875
•DOG FRIENDLINESS•	Can mostly run free, Carby Hill not good for older dogs
•PARKING•	Douglas Square
•PUBLIC TOILETS•	Langholm Street, next to fire station

BACKGROUND TO THE WALK

It might seem quiet today, but the area around Newcastleton was once what tabloid newspapers would now describe as 'war-torn'. Ownership of these borderlands was hotly disputed between England and Scotland for hundreds of years and there were frequent battles and skirmishes. You'll pass a reminder of those turbulent days on this walk.

Raids and Revenge

Because places like Newcastleton were so remote from the centres of power in both London and Edinburgh, they were not only difficult to defend, they also had a reputation for lawlessness. Feuds often developed between powerful local families and violent raids, and cases of cattle rustling (reiving), were common – cattle were then a valuable asset. These were ruthless people who could probably have shown the Vikings a thing or two about raping and pillaging.

A raid would commonly be followed by an illegal revenge attack (which of course was better fun, being illegal) or sometimes a legal 'Hot Trod'. This was a pursuit mounted immediately after a raid and had strict rules – including one stating that a lighted turf had to be carried if the trod crossed the border. When reivers were caught they were often taken hostage (the ransom money was very handy), taken prisoner, or even killed. Not surprisingly the countryside became studded with sturdy castles and fortified 'pele' towers, so that people could better defend themselves.

The most powerful family in this area were the Armstrongs, the principal reiving clan in the Borders. They were extremely influential and held large tracts of land. Their main seat was Mangerton Tower, the rather pitiful remains of which you can see on this walk. The Armstrongs were said to be able to muster 3,000 mounted men whenever they wished to launch a raid into England. They were ruthless and violent, running a rather successful protection racket as one of their money-making ventures. Imagine the mafia with cows and you'll get the picture.

Controlling the Clans

It wasn't until the Union of the Crowns took place in 1603, following the death of Queen Elizabeth I, that the Border wars ceased and the power of the reiving clans was finally dispersed. Keen to gain control and make his mark as an effective ruler of the new united kingdom, James VI of Scotland (James I of England) banned weapons and established mounted forces to police the area. Reiving families – often identified with the help of local informers – were scattered and members transported or even executed.

After Archibald Armstrong of Mangerton was executed in 1610, the Armstrongs lost their lands to the Scotts, another powerful local family. However, the family didn't disappear and members of this once fearsome tribe have continued to make their mark on the world. Most famous of all must be Neil Armstrong, who carried a fragment of Armstrong tartan when he stepped on to the surface of the moon, in 1969.

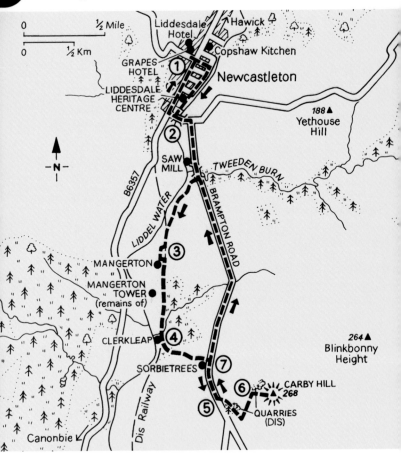

Walk 44 Directions

① From **Douglas Square**, with your back to the **Grapes Hotel**, walk along **Wyitchester Street** (or any other street opposite) and go down to the **Liddel Water**. Turn right, walk along the riverbank and join the path downstream to reach the bridge. Turn left at the top of the steps and cross the bridge.

② After about 100yds (91m), turn right and follow the **Brampton Road**, passing static caravans on either side. You'll eventually pass an old sawmill with a corrugated iron roof and will then reach the **Tweeden Burn bridge**. Cross the bridge and walk uphill, then turn right and join the metalled track that leads to **Mangerton farm**. Continue on this road until you near the farm buildings.

WHERE TO EAT AND DRINK ⓘ

You've got a few choices in Newcastleton. There's the **Grapes Hotel** on Douglas Square or the **Liddesdale Hotel,** also on Douglas Square, both of which serve bar meals. You can also try the **Copshaw Kitchen**, a coffee shop and licensed restaurant, which is on North Hermitage Street.

---

③ You now turn left, then sharp right, and walk down on to the bed of the old railway line, which has joined you from the right. This line once linked Carlisle to Edinburgh but was closed following the Beeching cuts of 1963. Follow the line as it leads past the remains of **Mangerton Tower**, in a field to your right, and continue until you reach **Clerkleap cottage**.

④ Turn left immediately after the cottage, then go through the

---

WHAT TO LOOK FOR ⓘ

You'll probably notice plenty of **stinging nettles** as you walk along the old railway line. That's because they love to grow on disturbed ground and flourish in environments such as this. They're a real favourite of **butterflies** such as the red admiral as they provide a juicy source of food for their caterpillars.

---

wooden gate to join a rough track. This leads through woodland and on, uphill, to join the road by **Sorbietrees farm**. Turn right now and walk along the road, past the farm, to a small stand of conifers on the left. Turn left through the gate.

⑤ Bear right now and head up the left-hand side of the trees. Walk past the top of the wood and a former quarry, to reach a dry-stone wall. Turn left and follow the wall uphill, crossing it about 437yds (400m) ahead at a convenient right-angle bend.

⑥ It's a bit of a scramble now, over bracken and scree, to reach the summit – the views are great though. Known locally as **Caerba Hill**, this was once the site of a prehistoric settlement. You now have to retrace your steps to reach the road again, then turn right and walk back to **Sorbietrees farm**.

WHILE YOU'RE THERE ⓘ

Liddesdale Heritage Centre and Museum is the place to come to learn more about the history of the area and its people. Trainspotters will love the Waverley Line memorabilia, which includes a seat from the station platform and an old railway clock. And if you're trying to trace your family tree you can make use of their genealogical records.

---

⑦ At the farm, continue on the main road as it bears right and follow it back over the **Tweeden bridge** and up to the **Holm Bridge**. Cross the bridge and walk straight on for 100yds (91m), then turn right on to the **B6357** and walk back to the village square via the little **heritage centre**.

Holy Orders at Jedburgh

Follow waymarked footpaths from this historic town.

•DISTANCE•	4½ miles (7.2km)
•MINIMUM TIME•	3hrs
•ASCENT / GRADIENT•	295ft (90m) ▲▲▲
•LEVEL OF DIFFICULTY•	🚶🚶 🚶🚶 🚶🚶
•PATHS•	Tracks, meadow paths and some sections of road, 2 stiles
•LANDSCAPE•	Gentle hills and fine old abbey
•SUGGESTED MAP•	aqua3 OS Explorer OL16 The Cheviot Hills
•START / FINISH•	Grid reference: NT 651204
•DOG FRIENDLINESS•	Fair, but keep on lead near sheep and on road
•PARKING•	Main car park by tourist information centre
•PUBLIC TOILETS•	At car park

BACKGROUND TO THE WALK

Although it was built back in the 12th century, the beauty and grandeur of Jedburgh Abbey is still clearly evident. It certainly dominates this bustling border town, and sits serene and seemingly untroubled by the hustle and hassle of modern life. It must have seemed still more impressive in medieval times, when the power of the Church was at its height and the population was generally uneducated and superstitious.

The abbey is one of four in the Borders – the others being at Dryburgh, Kelso and Melrose – and all were built after the Norman Conquest. They are stretched across the Borders like a string of ecclesiastical jewels. Jedburgh Abbey is one of the most impressive medieval buildings in Scotland. It was built for French Augustinian canons in 1138 by David I, on the site of an earlier Anglo-Saxon monastery, and was specifically designed to make a visual impact. This was not because the King was exceedingly devout, but was owing to the fact that Jedburgh is very close to the border with England. David needed to make an obvious statement of authority to his powerful Norman neighbours.

Monastic Life

Each of the Border abbeys belonged to a different religious order. The Augustinian canons at Jedburgh were also known as 'Black Canons' owing to the colour of their robes. Unlike monks, canons were all ordained clergymen who were allowed to administer Holy Communion. Dryburgh Abbey was founded by Premonstratensian (try saying that when you've had a few refreshments) canons, who wore white robes and lived a more secluded life than the Augustinians. Kelso Abbey, which became one of the largest monasteries in Scotland, belonged to the Benedictine order, while Melrose was founded by Cistercian monks. The Cistercians took their name from the forest of Cîteaux in France, where their first community was established. Often known as 'White Benedictines', Cistercian monks adhered strictly to the Rule of St Benedict. Manual labour in the abbey was carried out by poor, and generally illiterate, lay brothers. These people lived and worshipped separately to the 'choir' monks who devoted their time to reading, writing and private prayer. The Cistercians adhered to a strict regime, designed to purify their lives. They banned the use of bedspreads, combs and even underwear.

Abbeys Under Fire

These medieval abbeys all suffered in the battles that ravaged the Borders for centuries. Jedburgh, for example, was stripped of its roofing lead by Edward I's troops who stayed here during the Wars of Independence. It came under attack many times and was burned by the Earl of Surrey in 1530. After the Reformation, all the abbeys fell into decline and began to decay. Today they remain picturesque reminders of a previous age.

Walk 45 **Directions**

① From the car park, walk back to the **A68**. Turn right, then cross over before you reach the river. Take the

path on the left to walk beside the river, under an old bridge, then come on to the road. Cross and join the road opposite. Take the first right turn, then turn right at the **fire station** and cross the bridge.

Walk 45

② Turn left, following the sign for the Borders Abbeys Way. Where the road divides, turn left and walk beside the river again – there's a small 'W' waymarker. When you reach the main road, cross over and walk along the tarmac road. Keep going until you reach a large building on your left (it was derelict at the time of writing).

WHILE YOU'RE THERE ⓘ

In the town centre you can visit **Mary, Queen of Scots House**, a 16th-century fortified house where she stayed while visiting Jedburgh in 1566. She stayed here for several weeks recovering from a severe illness, caught following a lengthy moorland ride to Hermitage Castle, where she went to visit her injured lover, the Earl of Bothwell. Years later she regretted the fact that she hadn't died in Jedburgh.

---

③ Turn right here to walk in front of a small farmhouse called **Woodend**. When you reach another tarmac road, turn left. Your route now runs uphill, taking you past a radio mast and in front of **Mount Ulston house**. Maintain direction to join the narrow grassy track – this can get very muddy, even in the summer.

④ Squelch along this track until you reach the fingerpost at the end, where you turn left to join **St Cuthbert's Way**. The going becomes much easier now as it's a wide, firm track. When you reach

---

WHERE TO EAT AND DRINK ⓘ

Simply Scottish on the High Street in Jedburgh is a good licensed bistro with cheery yellow walls, pine tables and wooden floors. As well as serving lunches such as ploughman's, it also serves fresh scones, hearty breakfasts and more substantial meals in the evening.

---

the tarmac road, turn right and join the main road. Turn left, go over the bridge, then cross the road and go down some steps to continue following St Cuthbert's Way.

⑤ You're now on a narrow, grassy track which runs beside the river. You then have to nip over a couple of stiles, before walking across a meadow frequently grazed by sheep. Walk past the weir, then go through the gate to cross the suspension bridge – take care as it can get extremely slippery.

⑥ You now pass a sign for **Monteviot House** and walk through the woods to reach a fingerpost, where you can turn right to enjoy views over the river. If you wish to extend your walk, you can continue along St Cuthbert's Way until it joins the road, then retrace your steps. Whatever you choose, you then retrace your steps back over the suspension bridge, along the riverside and back to the main road. Cross over and rejoin the tarmac track.

WHAT TO LOOK FOR ⓘ

Monteviot House Gardens are open to the public from around April to October. There's a River Garden, with views over the Teviot; a walled Rose Garden, a Herb Garden and a Water Garden made of islands which are linked by bridges. If it's raining you can always take shelter in the large greenhouse.

---

⑦ The track almost immediately forks and you now turn right, following the road all the way back to join the **A68** once again. When you reach the road, turn left and follow it back into **Jedburgh**. Eventually you'll come to the car park on the left-hand side, which was the starting point of the walk.

One of Scotland's Great Scotts at Dryburgh

A gentle walk in the Borders countryside that was much beloved by that great national figure, Sir Walter Scott.

•DISTANCE•	4½ miles (7.2km)
•MINIMUM TIME•	1hr 30min
•ASCENT / GRADIENT•	131ft (40m) ▲ ▲ ▲
•LEVEL OF DIFFICULTY•	🚶 🚶 🚶
•PATHS•	Firm woodland and riverside tracks, 3 stiles
•LANDSCAPE•	Historic abbey and riverbanks
•SUGGESTED MAP•	aqua3 OS Explorer 338 Galashiels, Selkirk & Melrose
•START / FINISH•	Grid reference: NT 592318
•DOG FRIENDLINESS•	Keep on lead on Mertoun Estate and by golf course
•PARKING•	Dryburgh Abbey car park
•PUBLIC TOILETS•	At car park

BACKGROUND TO THE WALK

Walk anywhere in the Borders and you are probably following in the footsteps of one of Scotland's most celebrated literary figures – Sir Walter Scott. He travelled widely here and was celebrated during his lifetime, writing books that would be described as bestsellers if they were published today. Yet, while everyone has heard of Sir Walter Scott, hardly anyone now reads his books.

Wavering over *Waverley*

The reason for this is almost certainly the somewhat impenetrable nature of the language he uses – impenetrable to non Scots, anyway. Full of enthusiasm, people tend to pick up a copy of *Waverley* (1814), a romantic tale of the Jacobite rebellion, then put it down in defeat after page ten. But those that persist and learn to unravel the old Scots dialect discover tales that were strongly influenced by the ballads, folklore and history of the borderlands – tales that would have died out otherwise.

From Polio to Poetry

Scott was the son of an Edinburgh lawyer but spent a lot of time in the Borders as a child while recuperating from polio. He was fascinated by the stories and ballads he heard and, when he grew older, began to collect material that he later turned into romantic poetry. He was greatly influenced by Robert Burns and became friends with James Hogg, the Ettrick Shepherd. Scott became a barrister in 1792, but spent his spare time writing poetry. He was appointed Sheriff-Depute of Selkirk in 1799 and in 1811 he moved to Abbotsford, a farmhouse near Melrose, where he lived for the rest of his life. He turned to novel-writing, declaring that 'Byron beat me' at poetry.

It was a decision that was to make Scott's fortune – but it was also, ultimately, to cost him his health. After the publication of *Waverley*, he produced several more historical novels, including *Rob Roy* (1817), *The Heart of Midlothian* (1818) and *Ivanhoe* (1819).

Walk 46

Doing the Honours

Scott didn't just write about Scottish history, however – he also played his part in it. His novels revived interest in Scottish culture, at a time when it had been in danger of disappearing. In 1818 he discovered the Honours of Scotland, a crown, sword and sceptre, which had been hidden in Edinburgh Castle from the time of Charles II. And a few years later he was invited to make the arrangements for George IV's visit to Scotland – the King entered wholeheartedly into the spirit of the visit and delighted the crowds by wearing a kilt teamed with some natty pink tights.

Scott should have been able to relax and live in comfort, but in 1825 his publishing house collapsed and he was left with enormous debts. His wife died the same year. Scott worked furiously to pay off his debts, but his health suffered and in 1832 he died at Abbotsford. He is buried in the ruins of Dryburgh Abbey.

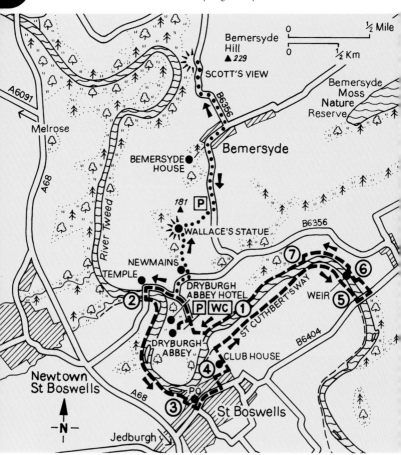

Walk 46 **Directions**

① From the car park at the abbey walk back to join the road, pass the entrance to the **Dryburgh Abbey** **Hotel**, then walk down the road in front of you. You'll soon see the river and will then pass a small temple in the trees on the right-hand side. Go left and cross the bridge over the **River Tweed**.

② Turn left immediately and join the **St Cuthbert's Way**. This waymarked trail now takes you along the banks of the river. At some points there are steps, tiny footbridges and patches of boardwalk to assist you. Continue to follow this trail which eventually takes you past two small islands in the river, where it then leads away from the riverbank.

③ Follow the trail on to a tarmac track, bear right and then left. At the main road in **St Boswells** go left again and continue to follow the trail signs, passing a **post office** and later Scott's View chippy on your left. After house No 101, turn left then go to your right along a tarmac track at the end.

WHILE YOU'RE THERE ⓘ

Abbotsford, west of Melrose, was Sir Walter Scott's home from 1811 until his death. He spent an enormous amount of money turning the original farmhouse into the home you see today. Scott's influence can be felt everywhere, from the library, which contains over 9,000 rare books, to the historic relics, such as Rob Roy's gun. You can visit both the house and grounds and there's a handy tea room too.

④ Follow this, then turn left and walk past the golf club house. Continue walking for a few paces, then turn right and follow the St Cuthbert's Way as it hugs the golf course. You now continue by the golf course until your track

eventually brings you back down to the riverbank. Walk past the weir and up to the bridge.

⑤ Go up the steps and cross the bridge, then turn sharp left and walk towards the cottages. Before the cottages, go left, over the footbridge, then turn right along the riverbank to walk in front of them. At the weir, take the steps that run up to the right, nip over the stile and into a field.

WHERE TO EAT AND DRINK ⓘ

The **Dryburgh Abbey Hotel** has a bar and restaurant that is open to non-residents. However if you want more choice, drive into Melrose where there are several pubs and restaurants offering everything from French food to traditional Scottish dishes. Perhaps the best known is **Burts Hotel**, an 18th-century inn which serves good bar meals and offers a choice of 50 single malt whiskies.

⑥ Go left now, through the gate, and follow the indistinct track – it's overgrown with high grasses in the summer but isn't hard to follow. Where the path divides, go left to keep to the river – you'll now be on short, springy grass.

⑦ Follow the river, keeping an eye out for fish leaping up to feed from the water's surface. You'll cross a stile, then pass a greenhouse on your left. Climb another stile here, turn right, walk past the toilets and, at the house ahead, turn left and walk back into the car park.

WHAT TO LOOK FOR ⓘ

The nearby Eildon Hills are a favourite haunt of **buzzards**. The common buzzard is Britain's most numerous large bird of prey and feeds on rabbits and other small mammals. It's had a chequered history and was badly affected by the introduction of myxomatosis in the mid-1950s, which almost obliterated the rabbit population. Sadly buzzards are still often killed by poisoned food that farmers and gamekeepers put out to kill foxes and crows.

Walk 47

The Holy Island of St Columba

A circuit of Iona to the marble quarry and the saint's landing place in Coracle Bay.

•DISTANCE•	5¼ miles (8.4km)
•MINIMUM TIME•	3hrs 30min
•ASCENT / GRADIENT•	650ft (198m) ▲▲▲
•LEVEL OF DIFFICULTY•	🚶 🚶 🚶
•PATHS•	Tracks, sandy paths, some rugged rock and heather
•LANDSCAPE•	Bare gneiss rock and Atlantic Ocean
•SUGGESTED MAP•	aqua3 OS Explorer 373 Iona, Staffa & Ross of Mull
•START / FINISH•	Grid reference: NM 286240
•DOG FRIENDLINESS•	On leads near sheep
•PARKING•	Ferry terminal at Fionnphort on Mull
•PUBLIC TOILETS•	Beside Martyr's Bay Bar

BACKGROUND TO THE WALK

In the early summer of AD 563, a middle-aged cleric crossed over from Ireland with 12 companions and the intention of setting up a monastic community on the remote and windswept island of Iona.

Flight of the Dove

Columba (in Gaelic, Colum Cille, the Dove of the Church) did not intend to bring Christianity to a new country, indeed he had left his native Ireland under a cloud. It had started with a dispute over copyright: Columba had secretly copied a psalter owned by St Finnian of Clonard, and Finnian had claimed ownership of the copy. The dispute became more complicated when a young prince accidentally killed an opponent during a game of Irish hockey and claimed sanctuary with Columba. A battle followed, for which Columba felt responsible. It was in penance for these events that he accepted 'white martyrdom', or perpetual exile.

Irish Poetry

At the centre of Columba's settlement on Iona was a church of oak logs and thatch and, around it, huts for the individual monks. Columba himself slept on the bedrock with a stone for a pillow. Larger huts of wattle were used as the dining hall, guest house, library and writing room. The monks' lives consisted of prayer, simple farming and study, and here Columba composed poetry in Latin and Irish.

Celtic Calendar Calculations

Columba's Celtic Christianity spread from Iona across Scotland, and led to the Northumbrian foundation of Lindisfarne, with its rich tradition of illustrated documents such as the *Lindisfarne Gospel*. Here it came into contact with the Roman-style Christianity of continental Europe, brought to England by Augustine in AD 597. While the outward

Walk 47

dispute was on the correct hairstyle for monks and the way to calculate the date of Easter, it seems that the Celtic Christianity was more personal and mystical, the Roman more authoritarian. The Roman version eventually dominated, but the Celtic was never suppressed. Columba, never officially canonised as a saint, is venerated in Scotland and Ireland to this day.

Iona Today

Columba's church vanished beneath a later Benedictine abbey, itself heavily restored in the 19th century. But the spirit of Columba still dominates the island. From the low hill called Dun I, on the day of his death, he blessed the island and community. The monks grew kale and oats at the machars (coastal lowlands) of Bay at the Back of the Ocean (Camus Cuil an t-Saimh), over what is today the golf course. At the southern tip of the island is Coracle Bay, traditionally named as the saint's landing place.

'That man is little to be envied, whose patriotism would not gain force upon the plain of Marathon, or whose piety would not grow warmer among the ruins of Iona,' said the renowned English writer and critic Samuel Johnson, who visited the island in 1773. Today's Iona Foundation is ecumenical – tied to no single denomination of Christianity – and has restored the buildings within a tradition of simple craftsmanship and prayer. The grave of John Smith, Labour leader in the 1990s, lies in the north east extension of the burial ground.

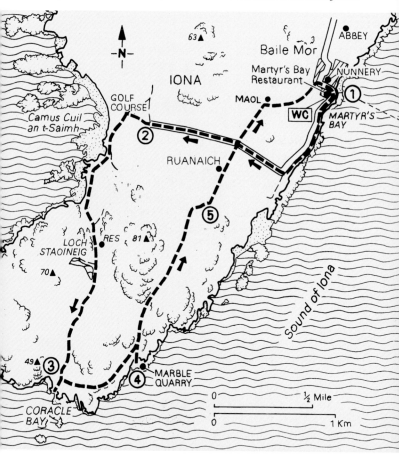

Walk 47

Walk 47 Directions

① Ferries cross to Iona about every hour. Once on the island, take the tarred road on the left, passing **Martyr's Bay**. After a second larger bay, rejoin the road as it bends right. Follow the road across the island to a gate on to the Iona golf course (dogs on leads).

② Take the sandy track ahead, then bear left past a small cairn to the shore. Turn left along the shore to a large beach. At its end, bear left up a narrow valley. After 100yds (91m) you pass a small concrete hut to join a stony track. It passes a fenced reservoir and drops to the corner of **Loch Staoineig**. Walk along to the left of the lochan on a path, improved in places, that runs gently down to **Coracle Bay**. You cross to the left of an area that shows the furrows of lazybed cultivation – fields drained to improve crop yields – and reach the shore just to the left of a rocky knoll.

③ The route ahead is pathless and hard. If your ferry leaves in two hours time or earlier, return by the outward route and leave the marble quarries for another visit. Otherwise, return inland for 200yds (183m) and bear right into a little grassy valley. After 100yds (91m), go through a broken wall and bear slightly left, past another inlet on the right. Cross heather to the eastern shoreline of the island. Bear

> #### WHERE TO EAT AND DRINK ⓘ
> On the island, you can try the **Martyr's Bay Restaurant** which offers fresh local seafood (March–November; dogs on the patio only). For a quick snack there's the **Heritage Tea Room** with its garden at the abbey.

left, above the small sea cliff, for ¼ mile (400m). Turn sharp right into a little valley descending to the remnants of the **marble quarry**.

> #### WHILE YOU'RE THERE ⓘ
> From Iona, or Fionnphort at the Mull end of the ferry, you can take an open boat trip to the island of Staffa to visit **Fingal's Cave** and its weird basalt formations. The crossing inspired an overture by Mendelssohn, but it isn't always as calm as the composer's dreamy sea-piece suggests. Take waterproofs and be prepared for a fairly bumpy ride – you're crossing the Atlantic, after all.

④ Turn inland, back up the valley to its head. Pass the low walls of two ruined cottages and continue in the same direction for about 200yds (183m) to a fence corner. Keep the fence on your left, picking a way through heather, rock and bog on sheep paths. Dun I with its cairn appears ahead – aim directly for it to reach the edge of fields, where a fence runs across ahead. Turn right along it to a small iron gate.

> #### WHAT TO LOOK FOR ⓘ
> The shingle at Coracle Bay has **cairns** (stone memorials) originally built by penitential monks. Over the years they have been renewed by visitors. Here you'll find greenish-white lumps of **Iona marble** among the grey gneiss. A long mound in the grass above the beach is supposed to indicate the dimensions of Columba's boat – 100ft (30m) long.

⑤ This leads to a track that passes **Ruanaich farm** to the tarred road of the outward walk. Cross into a farm track, which bends to the right at **Maol**. It reaches **Baile Mor** (the Iona village) at the ruined nunnery. Just ahead is the abbey with its squat square tower, or turn right directly to the ferry pier.

Into the Lost Valley

A rugged waterfall walk into the hidden hollow where the MacDonalds hid their stolen cows.

•DISTANCE•	2¾ miles (4.4km)
•MINIMUM TIME•	2hrs 15min
•ASCENT / GRADIENT•	1,050ft (320m) ▲▲▲
•LEVEL OF DIFFICULTY•	𝀝 𝀝 𝀝
•PATHS•	Rugged and stony, stream to wade through, 1 stile
•LANDSCAPE•	Crags and mountains
•SUGGESTED MAP•	aqua3 OS Explorer 384 Glen Coe & Glen Etive
•START / FINISH•	Grid reference: NN 168569
•DOG FRIENDLINESS•	Dogs must be reasonably fit and agile
•PARKING•	Lower of two roadside parking places opposite Gearr Aonach (middle one of Three Sisters)
•PUBLIC TOILETS•	Glencoe village

BACKGROUND TO THE WALK

The romantically named Lost Valley is 'Coire Gabhail' in Gaelic, the Corrie of Booty. Here, during the centuries leading up to the famous massacre of 1692, the MacDonalds hid their stolen cattle when the owners came storming in over the Moor of Rannoch with torch and claymore. It seems incredible that even the sure-footed black cattle of the clans could have been persuaded up the slope to Coire Gabhail. The corrie entrance is blocked by two old landslides from the face of Gearr Aonach, the middle hill of Glen Coe's Three Sisters. Stream shingle, backing up behind the obstruction, forms the smooth valley floor.

Noble Profession of Cattle Thief

The economic system of Highland Scotland, until the end of the clans in 1745, was based on the keeping and the stealing of cattle. It was an unsettled and dangerous lifestyle, and its artform was the verse of the bard who celebrated the most ingenious or violent acts of thievery and kept track of blood feuds.

Raiders of Glen Coe

The clan, gathered under its chieftain, was an organisation for protecting its own glen and for stealing from its neighbours. The MacDonalds of Glen Coe were particularly good at it. They raided right across the country, passing the fringes of the Cairngorms to steal from the fertile lands of Aberdeenshire and Moray. In 1689, when Campbell of Glen Lyon was a guest in the house of MacIan, chief of Glen Coe, his cold blue eyes may have dwelt on a particular cooking pot. Twice in the previous ten years, MacIan had come raiding into Glen Lyon, dishonoured the women by cutting off their hair and, on the second occasion, stolen that pot from Campbell's own mother.

The Massacre

By the late 1600s, the clan and the claymore were being replaced by a legal system backed by the central government and its army. But because they were so good at cattle thieving, the

MacDonalds of Glen Coe continued the practice long after everyone else had, reluctantly, started to move into the modern world of cash. As a result, the government decided to make an example of them.

On a cold February day, a squad of soldiers arrived in the valley. Traditional hospitality meant that even its leader Glen Lyon, a Campbell and an enemy, was welcomed into the house of MacDonald. Five nights later, at a given signal, the soldiers rose from their beds and started murdering their hosts. The Glen Coe Massacre was either incompetent or mercifully half-hearted. Of the valley's population of 300, just 40 were killed, with the remainder escaping through the snow to the Lost Valley and the other high corries.

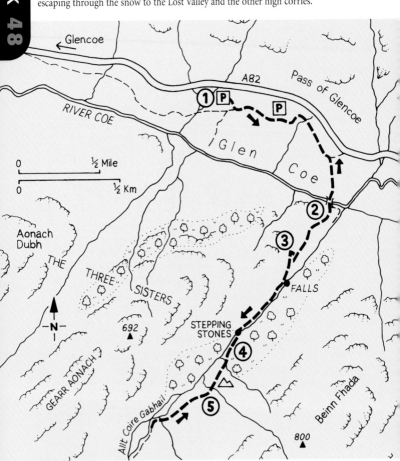

Walk 48 Directions

① From the uphill corner of the car park, a faint path slants down to the old road, which is now a well-used track. Head up-valley for about 650yds (594m). With the old road continuing as a green track ahead,

your path now bends down to the right. It has been rebuilt, with the bog problem solved by scraping down to the bedrock. The path reaches the gorge where the **River Coe** runs in a geological dyke of softer rock. Descend on a steep wooden step ladder, to cross a spectacular footbridge.

WHERE TO EAT AND DRINK ⓘ

The **Clachaig Inn**, on the old road to Glencoe village, has been the haunt of hill people for over a century. It serves hearty food, six real ales (one brewed from heather) and over 100 whiskies. The Boots Bar is well accustomed to tired and rather damp people coming out of the Lost Valley, though they do ask that boots be reasonably clean. Dogs are welcome, but children only in the more refined Bidean Bar.

② The ascent out of the gorge is on a bare rock staircase. Above, the path runs through regenerating birch wood, which can be very wet on the legs; sheep and deer have been excluded from the wood with a temporary fence. Emerge over this by a high ladder stile. The path, rebuilt in places, runs uphill for 60yds (55m). Here it bends left; an inconspicuous alternative path continues uphill, which can be used to bypass the narrow path of the main route.

③ The main route contours into the gorge of the **Allt Coire Gabhail**. It is narrow with steep drops below. Where there is an alternative of rock slabs and a narrow path just below, the slabs are more secure. You will hear waterfalls, then two fine ones come into view ahead. After passing these, continue between boulders to where the main path bends left to cross the stream below a boulder the size of a small house. (A small path runs on up to right of the stream, but leads nowhere useful.) The river here is wide and fairly shallow. Five or six stepping stones usually allow dry crossing. If the water is above the stones, then it's safer to wade alongside them; if the water is more than knee-deep the crossing should not be attempted.

④ A well-built path continues uphill, now with the stream on its right. After 100yds (91m) a lump of rock blocks the way. The path follows a slanting ramp up its right-hand side. It continues uphill, still rebuilt in places, passing above the boulder pile that blocks the valley, the result of two large rockfalls from under Gearr Aonach opposite. At the top of the rockpile the path levels, giving a good view into the **Lost Valley**.

WHILE YOU'RE THERE ⓘ

The National Trust for Scotland's new **visitor centre** is on the A82 opposite Glencoe village. (The earlier one, below the towering face of Bidean nan Bian, was removed in 1999 as an intrusion.) The centre tells the story of the glen, the MacDonalds and the Massacre of Glen Coe.

⑤ Drop gently to the valley's gravel floor. The stream vanishes into the gravel, to reappear below the boulder pile on the other side. Note where the path arrives at the gravel, as it becomes invisible at that point. Wander up the valley to where the stream vanishes, ¼ mile (400m) ahead. Anywhere beyond this point is more serious hillwalking than you have done up to now on this walk. Return to the path and follow it back to the start of the walk.

WHAT TO LOOK FOR ⓘ

Aonach Dubh is the right-hand of the Three Sisters of Glen Coe. High on its flank is the black slot of **Ossian's Cave**. Ossian was the bard to the Fingalians, a race of legendary giants who roamed the hills before the coming of the clans. His cave is hard to get to – a rock climb graded Difficult – and is most uncomfortable, as its floor slopes at an angle of 45 degrees.

Up and Down the Corrieyairack

Above the Great Glen on the road the English built and Bonnie Prince Charlie marched over.

•DISTANCE•	7¼ miles (11.7km)
•MINIMUM TIME•	4hrs
•ASCENT / GRADIENT•	1,300ft (395m) ▲▲▲
•LEVEL OF DIFFICULTY•	🚶🚶 🚶🚶 🚶🚶
•PATHS•	Tracks, one vanished pathless section, 2 stiles
•LANDSCAPE•	Foothills of Monadhliath, birchwood hollows
•SUGGESTED MAP•	aqua3 OS Explorer 400 Loch Lochy & Glen Roy
•START / FINISH•	Grid reference: NH 378080
•DOG FRIENDLINESS•	Off lead, unless passing sheep
•PARKING•	Southern edge of Fort Augustus, signed lane leads off A82 to burial ground
•PUBLIC TOILETS•	Fort Augustus

BACKGROUND TO THE WALK

The most striking feature of Scotland's geography is the 2,000ft (610m) deep Great Glen. It runs perfectly straight from Fort William to Inverness as if a giant ploughshare had been dragged across the country.

Scotland's San Andreas

Around 400 million years ago, the northern part of Scotland slipped 65 miles (105km) to the left. Looking across from Corrieyairack, you'd have seen ground that's now the Island of Mull. The Great Glen represents a tear-fault, similar to the San Andreas Fault in California, but no longer active, so that there isn't going to be any Fort Augustus Earthquake. Where two ground masses slide past each other, the rock where they touch is shattered. Rivers and glaciers have worn away this broken rock to make the striking valley.

Wade's Ways

After the uprising of 1715, General Wade became the military commander of Scotland. He constructed and repaired forts along the Great Glen at Fort William, Fort Augustus and Inverness, as well as at Ruthven on the present A9 and Glenelg. To link them, he built 260 miles (around 418km) of roads across the Highlands. The most spectacular of these was the one through the Corrieyairack Pass, rising to 2,500ft (762m) to link the Great Glen with the Spey.

The construction was little changed since Roman times. Large rocks were jammed together into a firm bed, up to 15ft (4.5m) wide, and then surfaced with smaller stones and gravel packed down. Modern path-builders know that however well you build it, if it's got water running down it turns into a stream. Wade paid particular attention to drainage. The 500 soldiers working through the summer of 1731 got a bonus of 6*d* a day – about £5 in today's money – and celebrated its completion with a barbecue of six oxen.

The chieftains worried that the roads would soften their people, making them unfit for raids across rough country. But they soon came to appreciate the convenience. 'If you'd seen these roads before they were made, You'd lift up your hands and bless General Wade.'

And when Prince Charles Stuart landed 14 years later, it was the Jacobite army that marched triumphantly across the Corrieyairack. At the Speyside end of the pass, a small and ill-prepared force under General John Cope fled before him into England. And a new Wade rhyme was inserted, temporarily, into the National Anthem itself: 'God grant that Marshal Wade, May by Thy mighty aid, Victory bring, May he sedition hush, and like a torrent rush, Rebellious Scots to crush, God save the King.'

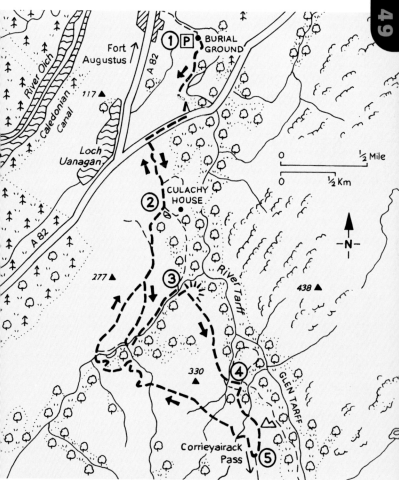

Walk 49 Directions

① A track leads round to left of the burial ground to meet a minor road. Turn right for about ¼ mile (400m) to the foot of a rather rubbly track signposted for the Corrieyairack Pass. After some 50yds (46m) the track passes through a gate, getting much easier, and, soon, the right of way joins a smoother track coming up from **Culachy House**.

② After another ¼ mile (400m), a gate leads out on to the open hill. About 350yds (320m) further on, the track passes under high-tension wires. At once bear left across a grassy meadow. As this drops towards a stream, you will see a green track slanting down to the right. Bear left off the track to pass the corner of a deer fence, where a small path continues down to the stream. Cross and turn downstream on an old grassy track. It recrosses the stream and passes under the high power line to a bend with a sudden view across deep and wooded **Glen Tarff**.

WHILE YOU'RE THERE ⓘ
You will find a rather specialised take on the life of the Highlanders at the **Clansman Centre** in Fort Augustus, which focuses on their techniques of doing away with one another. In a simulated turf house, staff will teach the 'art of killing or maiming using ancient weapons', and will even make the weapons for you themselves.

---

③ Turn right across a high stone bridge. A disused track climbs through birch woods then, as a terraced shelf, across the high side of Glen Tarff. A side stream forms a wooded re-entrant ahead. The old track contours in to this and crosses below a narrow waterfall – the former bridge has disappeared.

④ Contour out across the steep slope to pick up the old track as it restarts. It runs gently uphill to a gateless gateway in a fence. Turn up the fence to another gateway, 150yds (137m) above. Here turn left for 20yds (18m) to the brink of another stream hollow. (Its delightful Gaelic name – Sidhean Ceum na Goibhre – means 'Fairy Goat-step'.) Don't go into this, but

---

WHERE TO EAT AND DRINK ⓘ
The **Lock Inn** at Fort Augustus is not misspelled: its upstairs restaurant (April–October) overlooks not Loch Ness but the locks of the Caledonian Canal. Bar meals are served downstairs, year-round. Children welcome, but not dogs.

---

turn uphill alongside it, through pathless bracken, to its top. A deer fence is just above; turn left alongside it to go through a nearby gate, then left beside the fence. When it turns downhill, a green path continues ahead, gently uphill through heather. Far ahead and above, pylons crossing the skyline mark the **Corrieyairack Pass**. The path bends right to join the Corrieyairack track just above.

⑤ Turn right. The track passes a knoll on the right where a small cairn marks the highest point of this walk. It then descends in sweeping curves for 1¼ miles (2km). The pass is still technically a road, and where it crosses a stream, a Highways Authority sign warns motorists coming up it of the various difficulties and dangers ahead. From here the track climbs gently to rejoin the upward route. At the final bend, a stile offers a short cut through (rather than round) the ancient burial ground.

WHAT TO LOOK FOR ⓘ
Despite the road's preservation as an ancient monument, you will see little of General Wade's work, apart from its ambitious uphill line preserved by the modern track on top. You may be more interested by the **burial ground** at the start of the walk. Here is buried 'John Anderson, my Jo', subject of a sentimental poem by Robert Burns; and Gilleasbuig MacDonald, bard of North Uist, who died on his way to visit his publisher in Inverness.

The Pass of Ryvoan and the Thieves' Road

Following cattle thieves and drovers to the lochan used by the fairies for their laundry.

•DISTANCE•	5 miles (8km)
•MINIMUM TIME•	2hrs 15min
•ASCENT / GRADIENT•	400ft (122m) ▲ ▲ ▲
•LEVEL OF DIFFICULTY•	🚶 🚶 🚶
•PATHS•	Smooth tracks, one steep ascent, no stiles
•LANDSCAPE•	Views over Rothiemurchus Forest to Cairngorms
•SUGGESTED MAP•	aqua3 OS Explorer 403 Cairn Gorm & Aviemore
•START / FINISH•	Grid reference: NH 980095
•DOG FRIENDLINESS•	Off leads but under close control
•PARKING•	Bridge just south of Glenmore village
•PUBLIC TOILETS•	Glenmore village

BACKGROUND TO THE WALK

The Pass of Ryvoan has all the atmosphere of a classic Cairngorm through-route. It's a scaled down version of the famous and fearsome Lairig Ghru that cuts through the Cairngorm range southwards from Aviemore. You pass from the shelter of the forest to a green lochan, trapped between two high and stony mountainsides. Once through the narrow gap, you're in a different country. Here you will find wide moors and a ring of peaks around the horizon.

Thieving Ways

Ryvoan marked the exit of the Thieves' Road that ran out of Rannoch and Lochaber by secret ways through the Rothiemurchus Forest. The MacDonalds of Glen Coe used to come raiding here in the 17th century, as did Clan Cameron from Loch Eil near Fort William. Once through the pass, they could take their pick from the rich lands of Moray and Aberdeenshire.

In more settled times, the raiding chieftains became landlords, and their rents were paid in the small black cattle of the glens. Every autumn, the drove herds assembled for their long walk to the markets of Falkirk, Perth and northern England.

The Old Drove Road

The drovers used the same road as their thieving grandfathers, but once through the pass they turned sharp right across the flank of the mountain. The Lairig an Lui, the Pass of the Calves, crosses the dangerous ford of the Avon and runs down Glen Derry to Braemar. It's 30 miles (48km) to the next good grazing and shelter from the rain – two full days for the drove. Overnight the cattle would snatch some grazing from the rough grasses, while the drovers cooked their oatmeal and potatoes, before rolling themselves in their woollen plaids on a bed of heather. As late as 1859, Queen Victoria found the Lairig path torn up by hooves and scented with fresh cow pats.

The Sith and Others

Lochan Uaine means 'Green Loch'. Some say the green colour is caused by flecks of mica. Others claim that it's where the fairies wash their green garments. The Highland fairies, the Sith (pronounced 'Shee'), don't dance around with magic wands and grant you three wishes. They are touchy and vengeful, and if you meet one it is best to address him very politely in good Gaelic. Precautions you can take are to avoid wearing green, which is known to annoy them, and never to address your friends by name while still under the trees.

The Bodach Lamh-dearg is a spectre who appears wrapped in a grey plaid with one bloodstained hand, challenging passers-by to a fight and leaving their bodies for the foxes. Big Donald, the King of the Fairies, lived beside Loch Morlich. While wolves and bears may one day return to the forest, we should be more alarmed about the return of the Sith.

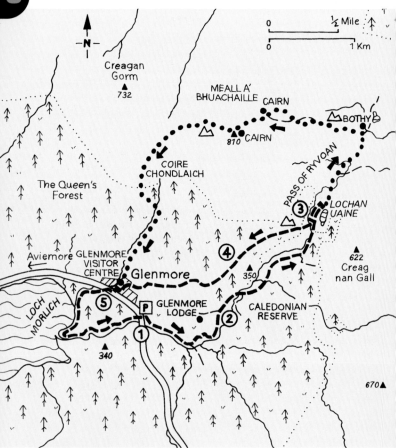

Walk 50 **Directions**

① Head upstream on a sandy track to the left of the river. Interpretation signs explain the flowers of the forest you may come across, many of which are ferns and mosses. After 550yds (503m), turn left on a wide smooth path with blue/yellow waymarkers. Ahead is a gate into **Glenmore Lodge** rifle range; here the path bends right, to a wide gravel track.

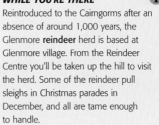

② Turn right, away from Glenmore Lodge, to cross a concrete bridge into the **Caledonian Reserve**. Immediately keep ahead on a smaller track (marked by a blue waymarker) as the main one bends right. The track narrows as it heads into the **Pass of Ryvoan** between steep wooded slopes of pine, birch and scree. At a sign that warns of the end of waymarking, a path turns left, with a blue waymarker, which you take in a moment. Just beyond this, steps on the right lead down to **Lochan Uaine**. Walk round to left of the water on the beach. At the head of the loch a small path leads back up to the track. Turn sharp left, back to the junction already visited; now turn off to the right on to the narrower path with the blue waymarker.

③ This small path crosses some duckboard and heads back down the valley. Very soon it starts to climb steeply to the right, up rough stone steps. When it levels off the going is easier, although it's still narrow with tree roots. The path reaches a forest road at a bench and a waymarker.

> **WHERE TO EAT AND DRINK** ⓘ
> The Forestry Commission's visitor centre has a café serving baked potatoes and snacks. Across the road, the **Glenmore Café** offers chips, toasties and red squirrels – the squirrels are outside, using a feeder placed directly opposite the windows.

④ Continue to the left along the track. After a clear-felled area with views, the track re-enters trees and slopes downhill into Glenmore village. Just above the main road turn right, through a green barrier, to reach **Glenmore Visitor Centre**. Pass through its car park to the main road.

> **WHILE YOU'RE THERE** ⓘ
> Reintroduced to the Cairngorms after an absence of around 1,000 years, the Glenmore **reindeer** herd is based at Glenmore village. From the Reindeer Centre you'll be taken up the hill to visit the herd. Some of the reindeer pull sleighs in Christmas parades in December, and all are tame enough to handle.

⑤ Cross to **Glenmore shop** with its café. Behind a red post-box, steps lead down to the campsite. Pass along its right-hand edge to a wide smooth path into birch woods (blue/brown waymarkers). Head left across a footbridge to the shore of **Loch Morlich** and follow the shore's sandy beaches (or paths in the woods on the left) until another river blocks the way. Turn left along the riverbank. Ignore a footbridge, but continue on the wide path (following brown/blue waymarkers) with the river on your right. Where the path divides, the smaller branch, with blue waymarkers, continues beside the river through broom bushes to the car park at the start of the walk.

> **WHAT TO LOOK FOR** ⓘ
> Elsewhere in Britain, **red squirrels** are being supplanted by their big grey cousins which were introduced from America. However, the red squirrel's smaller teeth are better adapted to life among the pines, and it is widespread in the Rothiemurchus Forest. Typically they'll run up the side of a tree trunk facing away from you, but then you'll see them escaping through the branches overhead. Close up – as at the Glenmore Café – you may notice their vicious little claws and teeth and realise they're nothing more than fluffy orange rats.

Walk 50

Acknowledgements

Front cover: Entrance to Carisbrooke Castle, AA World Travel Library/A Burton